COMBAT AIRCRAFT

110 DORNIER Do 24 UNITS

SERIES EDITOR TONY HOLMES

110

**COMBAT
AIRCRAFT**

Peter de Jong

DORNIER Do 24 UNITS

OSPREY
PUBLISHING

First published in Great Britain in 2015 by Osprey Publishing

PO Box 883, Oxford, OX1 9PL, UK

PO Box 3985, New York, NY 10185-3985, USA

E-mail: info@ospreypublishing.com

Osprey Publishing, part of Bloomsbury Publishing Plc

© 2015 Osprey Publishing Ltd.

ISBN: 978 1 4728 0570 6

PDF e-book ISBN: 978 1 4728 0571 3

e-Pub ISBN: 978 1 4728 0572 0

Edited by Tony Holmes

Cover Artwork by Mark Postlethwaite

Aircraft Profiles by Chris Davey

Index by Fionbar Lyons

Originated by PDQ Digital Media Solutions, UK

Printed in China through World Print Limited

16 17 18 19   10 9 8 7 6 5 4 3 2

Osprey Publishing is supporting the Woodland Trust, the UK's leading woodland conservation charity, by funding the dedication of trees.

www.ospreypublishing.com

Acknowledgements

The author wishes to express his sincere thanks to the following people who provided valuable help in the realisation of this volume – Juan Arraéz Cerdá, Werner Bittner, Peter Dupont, Herman Dekker, Pieter Hooijmans, Bart Lammerse, Derek Lilly, Thierry Matra, Ruud van Ommeren, Thijs Postma, Prudent Staal, Kari Stenman, Horst Thürling and Thomas Weis.

Front Cover

Allied as well as Axis airmen were rescued by the seaplanes of the German *Seenotdienst*, although there were other than humanitarian motives for saving the lives of enemy personnel. During the afternoon of Friday, 8 October 1943, a Do 24T-3 of *Seenotstaffel* 2 scrambled from its base at Schellingwoude, just east of Amsterdam. Across the Channel, a similarly configured Avro Anson I, EG543, of the RAF's No 278 Sqn took off from Coltishall to search for two USAAF servicemen who had survived the ditching of an Eighth Air Force B-24H Liberator in the North Sea at position WJ.0909, some 65 miles east of Great Yarmouth. A fighter escort was provided for the Anson I – something the German rescue pilots often, as in this case, had to do without in the second half of the war.

Neither rescue aircraft found anything, and the Anson crew had to make do without their fighter escort, as the four Spitfire VCs sent aloft by No 402 Sqn, RCAF, from Digby missed their rendezvous with the Anson. The Canadian fighter pilots did sight the Do 24, however, and immediately dropped their long-range tanks to dive into the attack. All four gave bursts of fire, and the flying boat's two outer engines were set alight. Although the Dornier subsequently crashed into the sea from a very low altitude, none of its six-man crew was seen by the four Spitfire pilots (Flt Lt J A H G de Niverville, Flg Off W G Dodd and Plt Offs L A Moore and L Woloschuk) who shared in the destruction of the enemy seaplane. The German airmen remain listed as missing to this day (*Cover artwork by Mark Postlethwaite*)

Back cover

This rare colour photograph shows KK+UM, the eighth Do 24 delivered to the *Seenotdienst*, somewhere in the central Mediterranean whilst serving with *Seenotstaffel* 6 in 1942. The early Do 24N aircraft were still powered by Wright Cyclone engines captured in the Dutch factory. The white Mediterranean theatre band has been painted out. Note the crew sitting on the *Stummeln* (wing root floats), which were critically important when operating from rough seas (*T Postma*)

CONTENTS

CHAPTER ONE

AIRLIFT INTO NARVIK

During the morning of 12 April 1940 at the Travemünde flight test centre, on Germany's Baltic coast, the drone of 12 Junkers Jumo diesel engines filled the spring air as four flying boats in dark green splinter camouflage taxied out on an urgent mission. They were three test articles of the humpbacked, twin-boom Blohm & Voss BV 138, nicknamed the 'Flying Clog', and a prototype of the elegant, swanlike Dornier Do 24.

The two types were rival designs, having competed to become the Luftwaffe's next maritime reconnaissance flying boat. The BV 138, originally known as the Hamburger Flugzeugbau Ha 138, had an embarrassing development history – the first prototype had been incapable of flight and the second was still seriously unstable, both on the water and in the air, despite having been redesigned. The Do 24, by contrast, was the best-handling seaplane the Travemünde test pilots had ever come across. A version built for the Dutch navy was even better, or so they had heard, as it did not use the sluggish diesel engine the Reich Air Ministry (RLM) was fitting to its flying boats. Although fuel-efficient, the Jumo was heavy and short on power. In late 1937 the RLM's fallibility was further underlined when it selected the BV 138 over the Do 24, stating that 'Dornier should focus on its bombers'.

It was now two-and-a-half years later, and although the BV 138's worst problems had been ironed out, it was *still* not operational with the sea reconnaissance units of the Luftwaffe – to the detriment of the

Requisitioned from the Travemünde test centre, both Junkers Jumo-powered Do 24 prototypes saw action during the Norwegian campaign in 1940. Do 24 V1 TJ+HR flew its first transport mission to Narvik on 12 April, where it was captured on film moored in the damaged port by German war photographer Gerd Böttger (*Bundesarchiv 101II-MW-5618-02*)

Kriegsmarine. Three days earlier, on 9 April 1940, the *Führer* had launched the invasion of Norway. Although the bold operation had achieved success, things were not going well in Narvik, high up beyond the polar circle. A German landing force had taken the port but had then been cut off by Royal Navy vessels led by the battleship HMS *Warspite*, which had raided the Ofotfjord and sunk two destroyers and the supply ship SS *Rauenfels* (along with its cargo of ammunition and guns). General Eduard Dietl, commander of the 3rd Mountain Division that had seized the Norwegian port, was in serious trouble.

The most sensible way to airlift supplies into this mountainous area was by seaplane, and a makeshift squadron of long-range transport flying boats was formed on 11 April. The unit was equipped with three Dornier Do 26 transatlantic mail-planes and the three BV 138A-0s and two Do 24s present at Travemünde. The latter were little flown and poorly equipped, although the Do 24 V1 was armed with an experimental 20 mm Rheinmetall MG 204 cannon in a HD 151/1 turret. The Do 24 V1 was added to the mission schedule for 12 April on the suggestion of eager young test pilot Adolf Mlodoch.

Loaded with ammunition and medical supplies, and with machine guns installed in its open nose and tail positions, the Do 24 V1 took off from the Pötenitzer Wiek bay at 0915 hrs. The three BV 138s could not unstick from the calm water, however – a familiar problem for heavily loaded, imperfect flying boats in quiet conditions. After several attempts the 'Flying Clogs' returned to shore, and Mlodoch landed and follow them back in. Although the BV 138s' mission was postponed, Mlodoch and his crew volunteered to head north alone, despite poor weather en route and their navigation 'chart' consisting of an atlas sheet! It was already past midday when they took off for a second time.

Rather than flying the shortest route, Mlodoch chose to follow the Norwegian coastline, counting the fjords while flying low under the clouds. Almost nine hours into the flight, they were heading up the Vestfjord towards their destination when they ran into the battleship *Warspite* and its destroyers, which were quick to open fire on them.

Mlodoch pulled up into the clouds and broke to starboard, despite the risk of hitting the cliffs. Easing back down, he discerned another fjord and, in his own words, 'plunged into it rather than landed'. Unsure about their location – this was the Efjord – they ventured ashore, but a scared local family in a lone hut did not offer them any clues as to their whereabouts.

Fearing that they would be discovered, Mlodoch and his crew took off early the next morning, running the gauntlet of British warships and misty cliffs again before landing in another inlet –

The Reich Air Ministry preferred the troubled Blohm & Voss BV 138 over the Do 24. On the first day of the improvised Norwegian airlift to Narvik in April 1940 the BV 138A-0s at Travemünde could not follow the Do 24 V1 into the air. NG+UC is seen at Hemnesberget shortly before it was shot down on 14 May 1940 (*Arkiv I Nordland*)

the Tjeld Sound – just ten minutes later. Having ascertained their location from a shepherd, they taxied clockwise around the island of Tjeldoya and took off into the Ofotfjord. Short on fuel but otherwise unscathed, they finally arrived in Narvik's port at 1325 hrs, German time – only for the crew to learn that their load of cannon shells was useless as the guns had been lost with the sinking of SS *Rauenfels*. At this point *Warspite* and its nine escorts launched a second raid, which caused the sinking of the eight remaining German destroyers left in the fjord, while a Swordfish floatplane sank a U-boat. The Do 24 survived the battle with minor damage, caused by machine gun fire, according to Mlodoch's account, when British sailors in a motorboat attempted to tow the seaplane away.

Having patched up the bullet holes, the German airmen took off at 0328 hrs on 16 April, carrying two wounded naval officers and a PoW who was somehow thought to be a nephew of Churchill! Leaking diesel, they landed at Thyborøn, in Denmark, where they were able to refuel, before finally reaching Travemünde at 1549 hrs.

Mlodoch aborted a second flight on 19 April, the Do 24 V2 prototype having technical issues. However, he managed to reach Narvik the next day in the V1, which had by then been repaired. The load this time consisted of two tonnes of explosives and two demolition specialists, who were to blow up strategic objects in case of a German withdrawal. The Wehrmacht's position in Narvik would remain precarious for two months, and the two Do 24s were kept busy transporting urgent cargoes until the end of the Norwegian campaign. The V1 ended its days on 18 September 1940 when it had to make an emergency landing near Vardø, beyond the North Cape. From there it was towed into the remote town's harbour by a fishing boat and subsequently scrapped. The Do 24 V2 was eventually cannibalised for parts before it too was broken up.

Another photograph of the Do 24 V1 in Norway. Machine guns had been hastily installed in the open nose and tail positions, while an experimental MG 204 cannon was fitted in the dorsal HD 151 turret – the ultimate Do 24T-3 used a similar turret. During the V1's first mission, on 12 April 1940, Adolf Mlodoch and his crew had to make landfall twice and ask local people for directions to Narvik! (*P Staal*)

CHAPTER TWO

GENESIS

The Do 24 V1, photographed in the Bay of Lübeck during trials in 1938. The Reich Air Ministry would not reconsider its preference for the Blohm & Voss BV 138 over the Do 24 (*K Kössler*)

One of the great names of German aviation is a French one, for although Claude Honoré Desiré Dornier was born in Bavaria on 14 May 1884 to a German mother, his father was a French wine merchant. Having led the Zeppelin aeroplane division during World War 1, Dornier made his name with his flying boats, notably the giant Do X and the versatile Do J Wal (Whale). The latter was an all-metal machine featuring side-mounted wing-shaped sponsons or *Stummeln* contributing to its good stability in the water, and a parasol wing topped off with twin engines in push-pull configuration in a central gondola. Having military as well as civil applications, the Wal was manufactured in Italy to avoid Allied restrictions. In 1931 production moved to the German Dornier company in Friedrichshafen-Manzell, on Lake Constance. Do Js serving with coastal units of the new Luftwaffe were given the Do 16 designation.

The Wal was also the mainstay of the air fleet of the Dutch navy in the Netherlands East Indies (NEI), now known as Indonesia. Some 46 Wals, most of them licence-built by the Aviolanda company in Holland, saw service with the Naval Air Service (MLD). Their important role in the external defence of the vast archipelago was to patrol the sea lanes, acting as the eyes of the navy's fleet of submarines and light cruisers while operating from remote forward bases.

In 1934 Dornier started designing a more refined successor to the Wal, designated the Do 18. It was soon ordered for the expanding Luftwaffe,

although only as interim equipment. Both the RLM and the Dutch navy wanted a more formidable, seaworthy machine, the MLD's 'dreamboat' having a maximum speed of 196 mph (the Do 18s could manage just 155 mph) and three or four engines for good one-engine-out performance. The latter requirement ruled out a new American flying boat that largely fitted the bill – the Consolidated PBY.

Substantial contracts for up to 72 aircraft were at stake, and three manufacturers submitted proposals, with Sikorsky's apparently failing to impress the Dutch navy. The Fokker B.V looked good on paper, but it would have been difficult for the struggling Dutch manufacturer to have built such a machine as the company had still to make the transition to monocoque metal. From the outset the MLD favoured the Dornier P.14 design (the future Do 24), which was declared the winner in August 1935. The RLM, on the other hand, had already developed a preference for the rival Hamburger Flugzeugbau Ha 138 (Blohm & Voss BV 138), and the Do 24's development was only allowed to continue because the Dutch government signed contracts in August 1936 committing to the purchase of six aircraft and the acquisition of a production licence.

Four prototypes were laid down, the V3 and V4 being the first two Do 24K aircraft for the MLD, fitted with Wright Cyclone engines for commonality with other Dutch aircraft. The V1 and V2 for the RLM got low priority, and thus the V3 became the first to be completed, performing high-speed taxi trials on Lake Constance on 2 July 1937, piloted by Erich Gundermann.

The new flying boat featured an elegantly curved fuselage with a twin-finned tail similar to that of the Do 17 bomber, as well as Dornier's trademark *Stummeln* which removed the need for outboard floats. Fuel tanks in the sponsons and central wing section fed the three 880 hp Wright R-1820-F52 Cyclone radials on the parasol wing. The fuselage or hull was divided into nine watertight compartments and equipped for a crew of five or six, with two pilots in compartment two, a radio operator and a navigator in compartment three, a flight engineer in compartment four and an optional full-time tail gunner in compartment nine. Nose and dorsal gun positions were provided in compartments one and seven. Amidships, compartments five and six were fitted out as crew cabins, with five bunks allowing personnel to sleep in the aircraft when operating away from base – passengers could also be seated here. Compartment seven doubled as a galley.

Some pilots likened the Do 24 to a 'flying U-boat', but seaworthiness trials held with the V3 prototype on the North Sea in September 1937 impressed Dutch and German observers alike (*T Postma*)

The first Do 24 to fly in July 1937, the Wright Cyclone-powered V3 was delivered to the Dutch navy after barely three months of testing and was shipped to the East Indies before the end of the year *(T Postma)*

The 600 hp Junkers Jumo 205C diesel engines fitted to the Do 24 V1 and V2 prototypes were fuel-efficient, but heavy and unresponsive *(T Postma)*

The first flight took place on 3 July, and subsequent testing also proved to be successful. After two months the V3 was flown to Einswarden, on the North Sea coast, for seaworthiness trials on an actual sea. The Do 24's behaviour in rough conditions impressed observers of the MLD, whose 'dreamboat' had come true. Only minor modifications were required before the V3 was accepted by the customer as the first Do 24K-1 service aircraft on 15 October 1937, barely three months after its first flight. Ferry flights to the NEI were decided against for crew availability reasons, which meant that the V3 was shipped out straight from Hamburg in November instead, entering MLD service as Her Majesty's Flying Boat X-1. The V4 prototype first flew on 2 February 1938, becoming X-2.

With Japan increasingly seen as a threat to the NEI, the 'X-boat' programme was gaining importance as a major Dutch defence project, the total requirement eventually amounting to 96 aircraft. As licence production by the Aviolanda company in Holland took time to get under way, the initial order for six from Dornier was increased to 30 in 1939.

The Dutch enthusiasm for the aircraft was not shared, however, by the RLM. The BV 138 had already been declared the winner of the German seaplane competition in September 1937, despite the impressive seaworthiness demonstrated by the Do 24 as opposed to the serious stability problems that dogged the 'Flying Clog'.

Powered by Junkers Jumo 205C engines of only 600 hp (rather than the 880 hp Wright R-1820-F52 Cyclone radials used by the MLD aircraft), the Do 24 V1 first flew on 10 January 1938. The brief evaluation of the diesel-powered Do 24 that took place shortly thereafter could not reverse the RLM's decision. The Do 24 V1 and V2 were subsequently used as test beds for new equipment and engine cold start trials, until rising to the occasion during the Norwegian campaign as described in Chapter 1.

INTO PRODUCTION

The RLM's lack of interest meant that no German production capacity was allocated to the Do 24. This meant that, apart from the MLD's X-1 and X-2, the remaining 30 machines supplied to the Dutch by Dornier were built by the company's Swiss subsidiary in St Gallen-Altenrhein, also on Lake Constance.

X-13 performing at a Dutch naval pageant off Scheveningen Beach, The Hague, on 3 September 1938, with the cruiser *Sumatra*, two minelayers and a submarine in the background. This aircraft became the first Do 24 to be equipped with the advanced French SAMM dorsal turret, although a wooden mock-up is still installed at this point (*T Postma*)

When complete, they were towed to Friedrichshafen for test and acceptance flights. Like the two prototypes, X-3 was shipped to the NEI from Hamburg. However, from X-4 onwards, the flying boats were delivered through Holland, landing on the Oude Maas River near the Aviolanda factory in Papendrecht for outfitting with military equipment. They were then shipped to the NEI from nearby Rotterdam.

The three Alkan turrets originally installed in the Do 24 only held a single 7.9 mm machine gun each, but from X-13 onwards a Hispano 20 mm cannon in an advanced French SAMM turret was fitted in the dorsal position. In September 1938 the new weapon was flight-tested in X-13 from De Mok seaplane station on Texel Island. Bombing was also practised during this 'boot camp', the Do 24 being able to carry up to 2645 lb of external stores in a secondary bombing role. Earlier in the month the same aircraft had participated in a naval pageant off Scheveningen beach, in The Hague, to commemorate Queen Wilhelmina's 40th anniversary on the throne.

The outbreak of World War 2 did not halt deliveries to neutral Holland, and the last of the 30 Do 24s supplied by Dornier arrived in November 1939. This machine had been completed at Friedrichshafen as the Do 24K-2 prototype, featuring 1000 hp R-1820-G102 Cyclones, increased fuel capacity and associated strengthening to increase speed and range. This machine's MLD registration was changed from X-30 to X-37 because the Dutch production line was to switch to the new model only after seven aircraft, X-30 to X-36, had been built. Due to Europe being at war, the Do 24K-2 had not been tested in Germany prior to delivery. This took place in Holland during the winter of 1939-40 instead, the seaplane being based at an old ferry quay at Moerdijk.

Do 24 licence production in Holland was slow to get under way, since Dutch aircraft manufacturers still had little experience in monocoque metal construction. The work was split between De Schelde, which built the wings at Vlissingen (Flushing), and Aviolanda, which built the fuselages and tailplanes and then undertook final assembly at Papendrecht. Dornier engineer Otto Stellmann was appointed technical supervisor. Orders for 43 aircraft – all but the first seven to be completed as Do 24K-2s – were placed in 1938-39, taking procurement to a provisional total of 73 Do 24s.

The last Do 24s to reach the Netherlands East Indies are seen at the Aviolanda factory in Papendrecht, wearing the orange markings introduced on 1 October 1939. X-37 was the German-built Do 24K-2 prototype, shipped on 8 May 1940. Aviolanda resumed production on German orders, and more than half of all Do 24s were built on this site (*T Postma*)

The first Dutch-built aircraft, X-30, was laid down in June 1938 and completed one year later – four months behind schedule. The manufacturers blamed Dornier's tardy transfer of information for the delay. X-36 (the seventh Aviolanda machine and the final Do 24K-1) was accepted by the MLD in March 1940. X-37 (the single Dornier-built K-2) was the next flying boat to be shipped to the colony, having completed its test programme. Although the seaplane was due to be followed by the first Aviolanda-built K-2s, this was not to be. X-37 left Rotterdam on board the freighter *Kota Inten* on 8 May 1940 – less than 48 hours before the German invasion of the Netherlands.

When the Wehrmacht entered Papendrecht in May 1940 it captured an assembly line of a quality German aircraft that, ironically, was not in production at home. Some 13 Do 24K-2s were under construction, and they ranged from 30 up to 90 per cent complete. Materials for more were in stock, and some 30 R-1820-G102 Cyclone engines were also warehoused on site. Stellmann had returned to his job before the end of May, and he duly ordered the readying of the most advanced airframes for German evaluation. This did not mean that the Do 24 was going to enter service with the Luftwaffe's maritime reconnaissance units, the *Küstenfliegergruppen*, after all. For one junior branch of the Luftwaffe, however, the sudden availability of the Dornier flying boat was like a gift from heaven. Indeed, the paramilitary *Seenotdienst* (literally 'sea emergency service') had only received its first aircraft during the previous summer.

Tasked with the rescue at sea of aircrew and – by extension – shipwrecked persons, the *Seenotdienst* had existed at military seaplane stations in northern Germany since 1935, using seaplane support vessels as rescue boats and reconnaissance seaplanes in the search role. Not until 1939 did exercises take Luftwaffe landplanes over the briny in any numbers, which

The pioneering German air-sea rescue service was initially equipped with the obsolete Heinkel He 59 floatplane. From 1940 it was slowly replaced by the Do 24, which soon proved to be formidable in the rescue role (*T Postma*)

Two captured Dutch Do 24s underwent operational trials from Norderney in the summer of 1940. *Seenotdienst* seaplanes were unarmed and painted as paramilitary Red Cross aircraft at this stage, but this soon changed as the British government did not recognise their non-combatant status and ordered the RAF to shoot them down when encountered (*T Postma*)

led to a decision to equip the service with aircraft of its own. The selected type was the Heinkel He 59, a large twin-engined float biplane, and an initial 14 were converted for the rescue role, receiving a rear fuselage hatch with a telescoping ladder and a hoist.

The cradle of the *Seenotdienst* (*Luft*) was Zwischenahn, a lakeside airfield near Oldenburg. From here, the world's first air-sea rescue squadron, *Seenotflugkommando* (SNFlKdo) 1, moved to the island of Norderney with three He 59s a few weeks before the outbreak of war. With a detachment on Sylt, it covered the German Bight, while in the Baltic SNFlKdo.2 formed at Bug, on Rügen, and Pillau in East Prussia.

The runaway German victories in the spring of 1940 meant that the waters to be covered by the service soon stretched from the Bay of Biscay to the Barents Sea. By the beginning of the Battle of Britain some 30 rescue-configured He 59s were available, with a few Do 18s also drafted in as stopgaps. The slow He 59 had serious shortcomings, however. Its range was on the modest side, and it could not take off or land in anything beyond sea state 3 (light). Moreover, it was not a particularly strong floatplane, and floatplanes are intrinsically weaker than flying boats anyway.

Seen here with Cyclone engines, KD+GJ was used as a development aircraft at the Weserflug company for the Bramo 323 Fafnir-powered Do 24T models (*T Postma*)

The Do 18 was not an improvement, though, and it was generally confined to the search role. It had long range, but its cabin was small and cramped, making on-board treatment of survivors difficult. Its seaworthiness was not that great either, and this was aggravated by its marginal performance, the Do 18 being another victim of the weak and unresponsive Jumo diesels. Its three-engined sister in its powerful Do 24K-2 form, by contrast, seemed tailor-made for the job – at least that was the opinion of the SNFlKdo.1 commander, Flugkapitän Karl Born, who paid a visit to the Dutch production line in Papendrecht in June 1940.

The first machine to be completed under the occupation, X-38, was flown to the Travemünde seaplane depot on 21 June 1940 for outfitting as an unarmed rescue aircraft. On 19 July it was sent to Norderney for operational evaluation as D-A+EAV. X-39 followed on 2 August as D-A+PDA, flown by Born, who also, according to his memoirs, demonstrated one of these aircraft to officials on the Schwielowsee, near Berlin. The Do 24's excellent suitability to the combat rescue role was confirmed by the former X-40, painted in full Luftwaffe markings as KD+GJ, in a test programme at Travemünde. Powerful, reasonably fast and roomy, the type had a radius of action of some 600 miles, with state-of-the-art navigation and radio equipment. Its behaviour in sea state 4 (moderate) was described as 'carefree', and with care it could land in sea state 6 (very rough, with wave heights of four to six metres).

Yet the adoption of the Do 24 in the rescue role was hardly a matter of course. The three-engined flying boat was a costly piece of equipment, a fully equipped example costing the German war chest one million Reichsmarks, notwithstanding the use of production facilities in occupied countries.

The *Seenotdienst* Do 24s normally operated with a crew of six, comprising a pilot, an aircraft commander/observer/navigator, a radio operator, two flight engineers/gunners and a tail gunner who, interestingly, doubled as a paramedic.

Pending development of a re-engined variant, the Do 2K-2 entered German service as the Do 24N-1, modified with two hatches on the port side to ease the taking on board of survivors. Eight rest bunks were provided in the amidships compartments, compared to five crew bunks in the Dutch aircraft. While standard German instruments were fitted, the Wright Cyclone engines were retained, although as the stock of Cyclones was soon depleted at least one of the thirteen or so Do 24Ns was flying with 865 hp BMW 132N radials by 1942. The French dorsal turret with Hispano cannon was also adopted, but a different tail turret was used, and MG 15 machine guns replaced the Colt-Brownings.

The former X-40, now KD+GJ, was sent to the Weserflug company at Einswarden to serve as a prototype for the definitive Do 24T, powered by Bramo 323 Fafnir radials of 1000 hp that could be boosted to 1200 hp for takeoff through water-methanol injection. The Aviolanda factory delivered the first production Do 24T in April 1941. Although only five aircraft were completed that year, approximately 240 Do 24Ts had been delivered by September 1944 when Germany ended the production of non-combat aircraft. While Aviolanda produced the lion's share, Fokker in Amsterdam delivered about 25, and 47 more were contributed by SNCAN (*Société Nationale de Constructions Aéronautiques du Nord*) in Sartrouville, near Paris – the former CAMS seaplane factory. SNCAN built 40 more Do 24s

for the French Navy after the country's liberation in 1944, raising Do 24 production to a grand total of approximately 330 aircraft.

Included in the Do 24T production were 11 T-1 and 38 T-2 aircraft, with the balance being Do 24T-3s. These versions differed in navigation and radio equipment, as well as in armament – the T-2 had a 20 mm MG 151/20 cannon in the dorsal SAMM turret, while the T-3 replaced this with a 15 mm MG 151/15 gun in an armoured HD151/1 turret. Later T-3s were fitted with 13 mm MG 151/13 machine guns fore and aft, and a FuG 101 radio altimeter landing aid was also introduced during the course of production.

The Do 24T was described as a rescue, transport and sea reconnaissance flying boat, but all production was for the *Seenotdienst* squadrons, which did diversify their range of duties in the course of the war, especially in the Mediterranean, the Black Sea and the Baltic. One Do 24 was tested as a minesweeper, fitted with a large electromagnetic ring around the fuselage in similar vogue to the Ju 52/3m MS and BV 138MS aircraft. Work on improved versions led to nothing both during and after the war, except that one surviving Do 24T was converted into the one-off Do 24ATT turboprop amphibian.

A new Do 24T-3 is run up outside the CAMS factory in Sartrouville, near Paris, on the Seine. The service history of this particular aircraft is unknown (*T Postma*)

CHAPTER THREE

X-BOATS

The first Do 24 to fly, the V3 prototype, arrived in the East Indies on board the Dutch freighter *Kota Nopan* in December 1937. It was now Her Majesty's Flying Boat X-1, the Do 24 having been allocated the type letter X in the MLD – it was often referred to as the 'X-boot' (X-boat). X-2, as the V4 prototype had become, was in use for crew training at Morokrembangan, the MLD's main base near the naval port of Surabaya, by early February 1938. In April both aircraft visited the colonial capital, Batavia (Jakarta), for inspection. Whilst there they flew members of the press and dignitaries, including the governor of the NEI. Fourteen Do 24s had arrived by the end of 1938.

In June 1939 a recent arrival, X-21, made an unpublicised reliability flight around the archipelago. Covering 7620 miles in five days, the route served as a useful introduction to the Do 24's vast Indonesian 'habitat'. On 1 June at 0100 hrs, the crew of Lt Cdr Van der Kroef and Lt Bakker departed Surabaya, East Java, and headed west for Sumatra, via Batavia. Refuelling at Padang en route, they eventually reached Sabang, the archipelago's westernmost city, after 1700 miles of flying. Day 2 ended at Pontianak on the west coast of Borneo. On the third day they overflew that rugged island to Tarakan, off the east coast, and continued to Ternate, in the Moluccas. Day 4 took them further east to Hollandia (Port Numbay). On 5 June they crossed the Dutch half of New Guinea to Merauke, overflying the virtually unknown Star Mountains range.

The flying boat then headed west, refuelling at Ambon, in the South Moluccas, and returned to Surabaya in the early hours of the 6th, having flown 2570 miles from Hollandia.

Rich in natural resources, including oil, this archipelago topped the 'shopping list' of the Japanese expansionists. The Dutch navy's strategy was to block the sea lanes with its 20 or so submarines, as well as a few light cruisers from its surface squadron. The MLD's long-range seaplanes fulfilled a vital reconnaissance role, deploying to forward bases in groups of three.

For crew availability reasons, the Do 24Ks arrived in the Netherlands East Indies by ship. X-1 is seen under reassembly at the MLD's main base of Surabaya-Morokrembangan. (*H Dekker*)

The first *Groep Vliegtuigen* (Aircraft Group, GVT) to replace the Wal with the new X-boats was GVT 3, which took X-10, X-11 and X-12 to Ambon for eight weeks in November 1938. Six groups with 18 Do 24s were operational by September 1939. Do 24 deliveries from Dornier and Aviolanda continued after the outbreak of war, but in May 1940 the shocking news of the German occupation of the motherland reached the NEI. The allegiance of the colonies to Queen Wilhelmina's government in exile in London was never in doubt. For the MLD this meant, however, that X-boat deliveries stopped after the 36 Do 24K-1 aircraft and one Do 24K-2, X-37, which arrived in Batavia on board *Kota Inten* on 28 June. Support from Europe was also cut off, and although maintenance facilities at Morokrembangan were comprehensive, a gradual erosion of the Do 24s' servicability set in.

With its different engines, X-37 was used as a training machine and as the MLD commander's aircraft. The first 12 machines were also preferably used for pilot training, as they had not had their dorsal 7.9 mm machine gun replaced with the 20 mm Hispano cannon. The ship carrying the SAMM turrets for these aircraft (the Dutch freighter *Tajandoen*) had been torpedoed by a U-boat in the English Channel in December 1939. The remaining 24 Do 24s equipped eight operational groups, six of which were normally 'op tocht' (on tour), with the other two undergoing

X-21 made a five-day reliability flight around the Indonesian archipelago in June 1939. It was fitted with a non-standard conical nose turret which impaired the pilots' forward view even more than the standard turret. The dorsal cannon turret had yet to be installed when the flight took place (*T Postma*)

maintenance at Surabaya. To make up for the undeliverable Do 24s, an order for 48 Catalinas was secured in the USA, with the first two aircraft arriving at Morokrembangan on 5 September 1941.

WAR IN SOUTHEAST ASIA

As war loomed on the horizon, the MLD crews kept themselves busy by tailing a fleet of 500 fishing boats operated by Japanese companies throughout the archipelago. Although an element of hysteria may have been involved, these vessels are widely believed to have been engaged in intelligence-gathering operations, as were Japanese diplomats and workers in other sectors of the NEI economy.

In early 1941 the Do 24s of GVT 2, based at Sedanau in the Natuna Islands, flew reconnaissance missions in response to reported Japanese troop concentrations on Formosa (Taiwan) – the likely starting point for an invasion of the NEI. The Do 24 groups were also active in a search for the raiding German cruiser *Admiral Scheer*, which made a brief appearance in the Indian Ocean. Military cooperation with the other Allies intensified, and one Do 24 group visited the Australian city of Darwin in May, flying there via Kupang and Broome. In July, Japanese troops occupied southern French Indochina (Vietnam), including the harbour of Cam Ranh Bay.

In early December 1941 the order of battle of the MLD's Do 24 groups, presented from west to east, was as follows. GVT 8 was based at Sambu Island, near Singapore, on request of the British, who were critically short of long-range reconnaissance aircraft themselves. GVT 4 was at Sambas, on the west coast of Borneo. GVT 7 was at Tarakan, in the Celebes Sea between Borneo and the Philippines. GVT 5 was at Ternate, covering the sea lanes through the Moluccas. In the far east of the archipelago, GVT 2 was at Sorong, in the Bird's Head peninsula of New Guinea, supported by the seaplane tender *Arend*.

Further south, a second echelon comprised GVT 16 at Batavia, equipped with Catalinas, GVT 6 at Morokrembangan, with Do 24s, and GVT 17 at Ambon, in the South Moluccas, again with Catalinas. Do 24 groups GVT 1 and 3 were undergoing maintenance at Morokrembangan, which was also home for two groups of antiquated Fokker T.IV twin-engined floatplanes and two groups of Fokker C.XIW shipboard floatplanes. Held in reserve and used for training were a number of new Catalinas, two Wals and ten Do 24s from the first batch of 12, the remaining two having been lost in accidents.

Outside Java there were only six true seaplane bases, mostly small and still under construction – Prapat, on Lake Toba, Sumatra; Pontianak, Tarakan and Balikpapan, in Borneo; Kalkas, on Lake Tondano, in Celebes (Sulawesi); and Halong, on Ambon. There were 51 auxiliary bases throughout the

X-19 was involved in the shooting of a Dutch navy propaganda film in 1939. Again, the dorsal turret is missing (*P Staal*)

archipelago, which had fuel stores and, in some cases, groundcrew, bombs or a radio station. There were an additional 153 landing sites marked on the pilots' charts, but these were undeveloped, being little more than dispersal areas. Seven militarised coast guard ships, converted to seaplane tenders, did enhance the long-range seaplane groups' mobility, however.

On 6 December two Do 24s of GVT 4 and GVT 8, and a Hudson of No 1 Sqn, Royal Australian Air Force (RAAF), discovered ships of a Japanese invasion fleet that subsequently landed troops at Kota Bharu, in Malaya, just after midnight on 8 December, local time – about 90 minutes before the first bombs fell on Pearl Harbor. The Dutch government declared war on Japan within hours, before the United States and Britain.

A formation takeoff of a Do 24 aircraft group from Broome during a visit to Australia in May 1941. Although the Dutch were now in the Allied camp, practical military cooperation was still exceptional (*P Staal*)

It was GVT 2 in remote New Guinea that was the first MLD group to see action. On 8 December the crew of X-12 spotted the Japanese schooner *Koukoku Maru*, with four small pearl fishing sailing boats in tow. Flown by Lt Adriaan Höfelt, X-12 bombed and strafed the ship, but no results were observed. The next morning X-11 and X-25 found and attacked the schooner again, and X-25 scored a direct hit with a 50 kg bomb, setting the vessel ablaze and killing ten Japanese sailors. The schooner sank later that day. Meanwhile, X-12 flew to Ambon – 280 miles away – to pick up fresh bombs.

On the shores of the South China Sea, the Do 24s of both GVT 8 and GVT 4 were due for maintenance at Surabaya – they were replaced by GVT 3 and GVT 1 on 10 and 12 December, respectively. Sambu Island was deemed too vulnerable to enemy attack, so GVT 3 moved to Tanjung Pinang, on Bintan (still closer to Singapore) on the 12th. The following day the Dutch Do 24s saw their first aerial combat when X-22 of GVT 3 encountered three Japanese aircraft. One 'fighter' was claimed damaged by the seaplane's dorsal gunner, Aircraft Machinist's Mate Leo Willems, although the enemy aeroplanes were actually Mitsubishi G3M 'Nell' bombers.

A few days later GVT 3 flew relief supplies into the town of Tarempa, in the Anambas Islands, which had been bombed and strafed by Japanese aircraft. European civilians were taken out on the return flights. On the 17th X-20 sunk a Japanese schooner, and on the 20th X-20 and X-22 were engaged in aerial combat with two of their Japanese peers – four-engined Kawanishi H6K 'Mavis' flying boats. X-22 was damaged, and had to be flown to Surabaya for repairs. The group's third aircraft, X-19, also had some skirmishes before GVT 3 was withdrawn to Surabaya on 31 December to start its conversion to the PBY Catalina.

On 12 December the three Do 24s of GVT 1 replaced GVT 3 at its base at Sambas, on the Sambas River in western Dutch Borneo. The unit flew its first patrols the next day, and on the 14th X-15 and X-35 encountered three enemy aeroplanes, with the Dutch crews claiming a dubious kill. The Japanese aircraft were probably Mitsubishi F1M2 'Pete' floatplanes from the seaplane tender *Kamikawa Maru*, protecting a force that had landed at the oil town of Miri, in British Borneo, on the 16th, thus starting the conquest of the island.

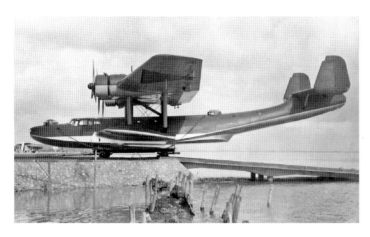

A fine photograph of a Do 24K-1 from the first batch in the colours and markings worn in December 1941. The X-boats had been repainted in a bluish 'mud grey', with milk white undersurfaces. The orange triangle national insignia had been downsized on the fuselage, although they were still large underwing. Upper wing triangles and orange rudders had been discontinued, and serials were applied in small characters below the tailplane only. This unidentified machine is seen at Surabaya–Morokrembangan. Seaplane ramps – not to mention cranes – were available in only a few places throughout the Indonesian archipelago (*Netherlands Institute for Military History*)

The Do 24 was often a solitary animal, but bombing missions by three-ship aircraft groups were flown on several occasions. GVT 7 bombed the Japanese invasion fleet for British Borneo on 17 December for example, sinking the destroyer *Shinonome* (*Netherlands Institute for Military History*)

The only Allied response to the invasion came from Dutch aircraft, including the three Do 24s of GVT 7 at Tarakan, off the east coast of Borneo, which mounted an attack with 250 kg bombs during the morning of the 17th. Off Lutong, north of Miri, three Japanese ships were sighted, and X-32, flown by Lt Bastiaan Sjerp, managed two direct hits on the destroyer *Shinonome*, which exploded and sank within minutes. There were few survivors from its crew of 228. Flown by Lt Jo Petschi, X-33 attacked a transport, inflicting only minor damage. The third Do 24, X-34, was reported missing – it had been attacked and damaged by another F1M2 'Pete' from the *Kamikawa Maru's* air wing. Pilots Lt Anton Baarschers and Sgt Jochem van Halm crash-landed on a river in Central Borneo. Two of the crew were killed, but the pilots and the radio operator, Seaman Klaas Auke Reen, hiked 120 miles through the jungle to the village of Long Nawang, which the Japanese did not reach until August 1942. The three airmen, and other westerners hiding there, were then decapitated or shot.

Meanwhile, off the west coast, X-36 of GVT 1 had landed near the Natuna Islands with engine problems on 15 December and been towed to Pontianak. While lying in the MLD base's floating dock, X-36 was caught in a Japanese air raid that killed 81 people on the 20th. Although the flying boat's centre engine was damaged in the attack, X-36 was flown out to Surabaya on two engines. It was replaced by X-6 on the 22nd. The next morning, this aircraft found a convoy of Japanese ships. A fighter, likely an F1M2 again, intercepted and damaged X-6. A short while later X-35 took off from Sambas to shadow the Japanese force, which was heading for the city of Kuching from Miri. Near Cape Datu, its crew, commanded by Lt Piet Jaapies, spotted a surfaced submarine that turned out to be the Dutch *K XIV*. Now the MLD crew could do what they had trained for.

By signal lamp, the submarine was informed of the convoy's position, heading and speed, and when the Japanese vessels launched two floatplanes, the X-boat went in and wiled them away to the northeast. That night, *K XIV* sunk the transports *Katori Maru* and *Hiyoshi Maru*, and damaged two others. Seriously damaged by the two chasing floatplanes, X-35 began to take on water after it landed on the river at Sambas. The crew was forced to beach the Do 24 so as to prevent it from sinking. The next day (24 December) this aircraft was also flown to Surabaya.

The 24th also saw GVT 1 move from Sambas to Tajan, inland from Pontianak on the Kapuas River. X-36 and X-35 rejoined the group just after Christmas, and X-6 returned to Surabaya. A mission was flown to locate the small British garrison of Kuching, which had withdrawn into Dutch Borneo and joined Dutch troops defending the

A Do 24 at Tanjung Pinang, on Bintan Island. GVT 3 moved here after the outbreak of the Pacific War. This photograph was taken prior to the conflict starting as the seaplane still has large orange triangles on the fuselage and orange rudders (*P Staal*)

strategically vital Singkawang II airfield. On the 29th X-15 encountered a patrolling G3M 'Nell' near Midai Island, in the Natunas, and was shot down. X-35 and X-36 fruitlessly searched for survivors for two days.

Although the eastern parts of the archipelago were still out of range for land-based Japanese bombers, H6K 'Mavis' long-range flying boats, operating from the Japanese trust territory of the Palau Islands, flew missions against Ternate and Sorong in mid-December, targeting their Dutch counterparts. On the 16th a 'Mavis' attacked the seaplane tender *Arend* at Sorong, but missed. X-12 and X-25 scrambled to give chase, only to discover that the Japanese flying boat was no slower than their Do 24. Guessing that the Japanese would come back, GVT 2 boss Lt Cdr Willem Reijnierse sent X-12 and X-25 up on a combat air patrol the next morning, with X-11 acting as bait on the water. A 'Mavis' suddenly popped out of the clouds, however, and it could not be intercepted. Fortunately, its bombs did not hit X-11.

By then GVT 5 had already left Ternate Island for a more secluded base at Kalkas, the newly improved seaplane station on Lake Tondano, near Manado, on the northern tip of Celebes. One of its Do 24s, X-30, was stopping by at Ternate, however, on the 17th when an H6K appeared and unsuccessfully attacked the seaplane tender *Poolster*. Flown by Lt Hugo Burgerhout, X-30 went after the attacker and, on this occasion, the Do 24 managed to catch up with the 'Mavis' after 30 minutes of flying at full throttle. X-30 was struck by several 20 mm shells from the H6K's tail gunner, however, knocking out its electric system and the centre engine. The following day X-30 was flown to Ambon for a quick repair.

BOMBING THE PHILIPPINES

On 20 December the Japanese seized the port of Davao, in the Philippines, which was subsequently used as a springboard for operations in the eastern half of the NEI. Not wanting to sit idly by while the enemy prepared for an invasion, Dutch Vice Adm Conrad Helfrich ordered a raid against Davao by two of his Do 24 groups, GVT 2 and GVT 5, for the morning of the 23rd. In preparation, GVT 2 flew from New Guinea to Kalkas on the 22nd. Since the base at Kalkas was only small, GVT 5 moved to Talisei Island, further north.

Inbound to the target, the three Do 24s of GVT 5 lost sight of each other while flying through cloud at night, although X-27 rejoined

Aircraft Machinist's Mate Bogerd points out a hit scored by the tail gunner of a *Mavis* flying boat against Lt Hugo Burgerhout's X-30 on 17 December (*T Postma*)

Members of Lt Hugo Burgerhout's crew – radio operator Murtamadji, Aircraft Machinist's Mate Bogerd and pilot Lt Van Leeuwen. Quickly repaired at Ambon, X-30 took part in the bombing raid against the Philippine port of Davao on 23 December, and on the way back rescued the crew of X-27, which had been forced down by enemy fire. The mixed ethnicity of the crews is of interest, although there was no doubt about who pulled the strings under Dutch colonial rule (*Netherlands Institute for Military History*)

formation with X-30 just as they reached Davao. Flown by Lt Burgerhout, X-30 dropped its six 250 kg bombs on the port's warehouses and quays, while X-27 targeted a group of H6K flying boats. Then the third Dornier, X-26, came in, missing a warship with its bombs. GVT 2 arrived overhead five minutes later, as planned, and its three Do 24s attacked and damaged the huge tanker *Tonan Maru 2*, claiming a direct hit on its bow. *Tonan Maru 2* was a former whale factory ship that had been requisitioned by the Imperial Japanese Navy (IJN). Its sister ship *Tonan Maru 3* may have been slightly damaged by *K XIV*'s attack off Kuching that same day.

GVT 2 returned safely to Lake Tondano, but X-27 of GVT 5 was hit by anti-aircraft fire that took out its starboard engine. The flying boat was then attacked by a patrolling 'Pete' from the seaplane tender *Sanuki Maru*, which holed the Do 24's fuel tanks and wounded the tail gunner. The latter almost certainly damaged the floatplane in return, as a 'Pete' crashed upon landing due to a perforated centreline float. The Do 24 was finished too, however, despite the crew using its bilge pump to bail leaking fuel into its only undamaged tank. X-27 set down on a rough open sea, at which point radio silence was broken and X-30 returned. Lt Burgerhout successfully landed in wind force 6 conditions to rescue the crew from their dinghies. X-26 and X-30 then safely joined GVT 2 at Lake Tondano.

The mission was considered a success, and the two Do 24 groups were kept together at Lake Tondao for a raid against a Japanese convoy. It was a risky decision, and X-30 was sent on a reconnaissance sortie towards Davao during the morning of the 26th. Then at 0710 hrs Lake Tondao was attacked by six A6M Zero-sens, which strafed the four remaining Do 24s there to destruction – a Sikorsky S-42 of the NEI airline KNILM was also destroyed. Six men lay dead as X-30 returned from its mission. The MLD base was abandoned and the surviving personnel from the two groups were flown to Surabaya by X-30 and a Catalina.

Meanwhile, GVT 7 was still based at Tarakan, off the east coast of Borneo, with two Do 24s – following the loss of X-34 in the raid against Miri, X-10 had been sent to the group as a replacement, but the condition of this aircraft was so poor that it was immediately sent back. While on patrol on 24 December, the crew of X-32 sighted a plume of smoke and found the American ship *Ruth Alexander*, which was escaping from Manila, under attack from an F1M2 'Pete'. The latter turned its attention to the Do 24, and in the ensuing fight the Japanese floatplane was damaged and its gunner disabled. Upon landing alongside its tender – the *Kamikawa Maru* again – the floatplane sank before it could be hoisted on board. X-32 sustained some light damage.

That same day the Japanese occupied Jolo Island, halfway between Davao and Borneo. All remaining Do 24s in the area were ordered to mount a raid against the ships of the landing force. However, with GVT 2 and GVT 5 wiped out at Lake Tondano on the 26th and X-32 under repair, only X-33 was available. Lt Petschi and his crew dutifully went in on the 27th and attacked a cruiser, but the lone Do 24 was in turn set upon by Zero-sens and seriously damaged by flak. The flying boat had to be flown to Surabaya for repairs the following day.

By the end of December X-32 had been returned to airworthiness at Tarakan, and whilst on patrol on the 31st it was called in by the lighthouse keeper of Cape Mangkalihat, Borneo's eastern tip. *Ruth Alexander* had now been attacked by Japanese bombers, forcing its crew to abandon the blazing, sinking ship. The subsequent rescue effected by the crew of X-32 was 'heroic' according to Peter Stone in his book *The Lady and the President*;

'The Dutch pilot of the Dornier ordered all his bombs and supplies jettisoned to make room for the 46-man crew of the sunken vessel. The only way this number could be accommodated was to have them stand upright, packed close together. Even the wounded had to stand straight up. The aeroplane's load was so heavy the pilot had to taxi five miles before he could get his ship into the air.'

On 3 January, as GVT 7 was relieved, X-32 flew to Surabaya, from where it mounted another rescue mission on the 9th, collecting 54 crew members of the Dutch cattle ship *Camphuys* that had been sunk by the IJN submarine *I-58*. The following day the Dutch naval tanker *Djirak* fell victim to *I-57*, and two days later X-32 picked up 38 survivors from Sepanjang Island.

As the IJN's submarines caused carnage among shipping around Java and Bali, Do 24s serving with the reserve pool and the flying school at Morokrembangan, including X-23 and X-24, joined the action. The American freighter *Liberty* was torpedoed by *I-66* near Penida Island at 0315 hrs on the 11th. Piloted by Sgt Eef Smitshuysen, X-24 landed alongside a raft and picked up 27 survivors who were dropped off at Benoa, Bali. The flying boat then returned to collect another 27 American sailors who were taken to Surabaya (*Liberty* was eventually stranded on the north coast of Bali, and today it is one of the easiest wreck dives in the world). On the 12th *I-56* was busy shooting up the steamship *Patras* in the Lombok Strait when the appearance of X-23 caused the submarine to crash-dive and run, even though the Do 24 was on a training flight – it was devoid of bombs or depth charges.

GVT 4 had relieved GVT 7 at the Tarakan base on 3 January. A site on the Berau River, 65 miles south, was used as a hideout as Tarakan was now within range of enemy fighters. The Japanese had immediately begun to improve Jolo's airfield, and GVT 4's X-13 attacked it with a dozen 50 kg bombs during the moonlit night of 9 January. The following day, X-14 and X-21 reconnoitred an IJN invasion fleet bound for Tarakan. Flying low along the Bornean shoreline all afternoon, Lt Cdr Simon Rosier popped up briefly when he sighted a mast top. His count was 37 ships, including six cruisers, six *Fubuki* class destroyers and one seaplane tender. Based at Samarinda II airfield, Martin 139 bombers of NEI Army Aviation were sent to attack the convoy, but no hits were observed by Rosier.

Tarakan's small garrison had already begun to destroy local oil installations and the seaplane base, while X-13 flew south to turn back a Dutch vessel transporting 50 soldiers from Samarinda. The vessel was hit by a bomb from a Japanese flying boat, however, and it then ran aground

Long, often featureless maritime reconnaissance and anti-submarine patrols exhausted the Dutch flying boat crews who were flying up to 18 hours a day (*P Staal*)

on a reef. X-13 rescued the wounded, and X-14 and X-21 picked up the remaining survivors as GVT 4 withdrew to Balikpapan.

On 19 January X-13 and X-14 sighted two white men on a motor launch waving a Dutch flag, and they were picked up the following morning by X-21, flown by Lt Cdr Rosier. The Japanese had sent the two men with a message, threatening mass executions if Balikpapan's oil rigs and refineries were not left intact. The city's commander ignored this threat, and oil tanks in the harbour were ablaze as GVT 4 left for Surabaya on the 22nd. Its three Do 24s and another returned to Balikpapan later in the day to evacuate the demolition squads. The weather turned bad en route, however, and while one Do 24 abandoned the mission, X-14 crashed while attempting to land, killing four of its crew.

Twenty-four hours earlier GVT 7, which had been sent back into action from Makassar, in South Celebes, had reconnoitred the landing fleet for Balikpapan. It then started shadowing the Japanese ships, which were attacked by Dutch Martin 139 bombers, Buffalo fighters and a submarine, as well as by four US destroyers. Six Japanese transports were sunk, but the landing at Balikpapan itself was unopposed.

At about the same time, the Japanese began their advance on the west coast of Borneo from Kuching. Here, GVT 1 had left Tajan on New Year's Day – it was relieved by GVT 6, which had spent the first month of the war flying anti-submarine patrols from Surabaya. The unit's commander, Lt Stegeman, was a thoughtful officer who managed to prevent losses by carefully dispersing his aeroplanes between flights, and by avoiding Japanese aircraft in the air – their daily reconnaissance missions following predictable patterns. But Stegeman also sought permission to bomb targets at Kuching while enemy air defences were still weak. Six missions were flown against Kuching's port, its airfield and the Singkawang road from 16-24 January. A few Japanese aircraft were claimed destroyed on the ground, and there was a huge explosion as an ammunition dump was apparently blown up.

At the same time GVT 6 still flew reconnaissance patrols over the South China Sea and also humanitarian missions. On the 18th the Russian steamer *Perekop* was sunk by Japanese bombers on its hazardous route from Vladivostok to Surabaya (the Soviet Union and Japan were not at war), and on the 24th X-29 flew four sick Russian survivors from Great Natuna Island to Pontianak. The following day rice was dropped for the people of the isolated Tambalan Islands. On 26 January a schooner carrying Japanese troops was left in flames after it was attacked by X-29 near Cape Api, although one of the flying boat's crew was killed by anti-aircraft fire. The Japanese were using a flotilla of such small vessels to land near Sambas and capture Singkawang II airfield. Raids against the latter by the three Do 24s of GVT 6 had little effect on the enemy, and left X-29 so badly damaged that it had to be flown to Surabaya on the 29th. X-23 arrived as a replacement. GVT 6 had left Tajan for Ketapang, further south, the previous day, but with the fall of the main town of Pontianak, this new hideout became untenable. GVT 6 withdrew to Surabaya on the 30th.

Banjarmasin, the last major objective on Borneo, fell on 10 February. X-29, which had been repaired, undertook an evacuation mission to the city the following night. The seaplane quickly drew enemy fire, and nose gunner Sgt Jan de Vries was hit in a leg. The aircraft commander, Lt Paul Adriani, aborted his landing. On the return leg two engines failed near Surabaya and the flying boat crashed into the dark sea. Half of the crew, including the wounded Sgt De Vries, went down with the sinking aircraft. The remaining three got out and reached Java in a dinghy, but Adriani succumbed to his wounds the following evening.

X-19 of GVT 4 had also crashed near Surabaya as it landed in a rice paddy during the night of 25 January, killing its pilots. In this case, crew fatigue was the probable cause, with the MLD airmen often flying 15 to 18 hours a day. Having only one aircraft left, GVT 4 was disbanded, leaving just three groups still operating Do 24s by 30 January. These were GVT 6 and GVT 7 at Surabaya and GVT 8 at Batavia–Tanjung Priok. GVT 1 had also been disbanded, and GVT 2, GVT 3 and GVT 5 had converted to Catalinas. Within the American, British, Dutch, Australian (ABDA) supreme command, the MLD's Capt Gerard Bozuwa was now in charge of the aerial reconnaissance aircraft group, which included a handful of US Navy PBYs at Surabaya and two RAF Catalinas at Batavia-Tanjung Priok. ABDA's longer, bilingual lines of command hampered cooperation between Dutch aircraft and ships, however.

On 31 January the Japanese took Ambon, the key to the southeastern parts of the archipelago. The previous day GVT 7 had been sent east to guard the sea lanes leading to Java between Celebes and Timor. The area was now within range of Japanese aircraft from Kendari, in Celebes, however, and the harbour of Kupang in Dutch Timor was too vulnerable as a base – various coves around the Sawu Sea coastline had to be used instead. X-33 was soon damaged in a heavy landing and flown to Surabaya for repair. It was replaced by X-13, which joined X-32 and X-35 at Rote Island on 7 February just as the group was targeted by an air raid. All three flying boats were destroyed. Surviving personnel were flown to Surabaya by Do 24s of GVT 6.

Meanwhile, Surabaya was also coming under air attack. Four Do 24s were destroyed there on 3 February and two more on the 5th. The MLD

Do 24s at the MLD main base of Morokrembangan, East Java, which came within range of Japanese aircraft in early February 1942. Six Do 24s were destroyed here in raids on the 3rd and 5th (*Netherlands Institute for Military History*)

flying school was moved to Australia, and five Do 24s of the first batch, used for training, were flown out on 19 February.

Do 24 X-17 of GVT 8 was based at Lake Toba, in Sumatra, from 25 January, flying anti-submarine patrols over the Indian Ocean. In early February it rescued 93 survivors of the Dutch steamer *Van Overstraten*, which had been sunk by the submarine *I-64* some 500 miles from the Sumatran coast. X-17 returned to Tanjung Priok on 9 February, X-16 relieving it at Lake Toba. Three days later X-17 and X-18 fought off two F1M2 'Petes' near Biliton Island. The enemy seaplanes belonged to an invasion force that had taken Bangka Island, with its seaports and airfield, and the oil town of Palembang, in southern Sumatra, by 16 February. Singapore had also fallen. Despite these important events, the crews of X-17 and X-18 were required to fly supply sorties for British Indian troops who had fled into the interior of Borneo to Sintang, on the Kapuas River.

The same crews encountered a Japanese destroyer in the Bangka Strait on 17 February, but they did not attack the vessel as they were unsure of its nationality. That same day the Dutch steamer *Sloet van de Beele*, carrying as many as 1000 evacuees from Biliton, and its escort, the destroyer *Van Nes*, were sunk by land-based G3M bombers and B5N 'Kates' from the aircraft carrier *Ryujo*. A rescue operation belatedly began on the 19th, and 358 people were rescued, the great majority by three Do 24s and a Catalina of the MLD. PBY Y-45 carried off an astonishing 79 survivors in a single flight.

On 23 February a flight of three Martin 139 bombers reconnoitred five or six small Japanese transport ships in the port of Muntok, Bangka, and attacked without results. Two RAF Blenheims flew a repeat attack, but they were forced to flee when intercepted by A6M Zero-sens that had just arrived at Muntok's airfield. Despite the presence of the fighters, X-17 and X-18 were ordered to fly another unescorted attack mission against the ships the following day, attacking individually. Both flying boats were duly shot down, X-17 probably by the locally based Zero-sens and X-18 falling victim to a flight of Ki-43 'Oscar' fighters returning from a raid on Batavia. GVT 8 commander Lt Will Aernout and his crew were able to swim to the Noordwachter (Jaga Utara) lighthouse. The crew of X-17 was killed, however.

The next day (25 February), on the other end of Java, X-21 of GVT 6 was also lost to Zero-sens over the Lombok Strait. Also on the 25th, a flying boat reconnoitred the Japanese invasion fleet for East Java at Balikpapan. The following day, X-28 of GVT 6 found it near Arendseiland (Pulau Karamian), and ABDA's naval strike force, led by Dutch Rear Adm Karel Doorman, sailed from Surabaya. The Allies lost track of the enemy in bad weather, however, and at this crucial hour, due to the overworked condition of both the flying boats and the crews, the reconnaissance group could only send up two or three seaplanes at a time. The Allied squadron was wiped out in the Battle of the Java Sea, Doorman going down with his flagship *De Ruyter*. On the 28th the Do 24s of GVT 6 sought fruitlessly for survivors from the sunken warships. Japanese troops landed in East Java at dawn the next day, with a second invasion force approaching from the west.

As the Japanese approached Java and Sumatra, X-17 and X-18 of GVT 8 flew an unescorted raid against transports in the port of Muntok, on Bangka Island, despite the known presence of fighters. Both flying boats were shot down and Lt Van den End and his crew in X-17 were killed. The wreck of X-17 was photographed by Catalina Y-64 (*T Postma*)

As a Short Empire flying boat takes off from Roebuck Bay, Broome, a Do 24 is seen in the foreground in this photograph, which was taken from another Empire 'boat'. This shot was dated February 1942, and it probably shows a flying school Do 24, rather than one of the 'last aircraft out' arriving from Java just before the notorious Japanese air raid on 3 March (*Aviation Heritage Museum of Western Australia*)

Only one Do 24, X-16, was now left at Batavia-Tanjung Priok – probably unserviceable, the seaplane was destroyed along with its hangar before the arrival of the Japanese. Morokrembangan was evacuated on 1 March, GVT 6 flying to Lengkong, a primitive auxiliary base on the Brantas River, and GVT 7, now with four Do 24s, to Lake Grati, near the Bromo volcano. Orders were received to proceed to Australia, and X-3 and X-28 of GVT 6 landed in Roebuck Bay at Broome, in Western Australia, early next morning. X-23 was delayed by engine trouble, and like Adolf Mlodoch's crew over Norway two years earlier, its young navigator, Sgt Rudolf Idzerda (who would eventually reach the rank of vice admiral) only had a basic map torn from an atlas. He ended up at nearby Port Hedland, eventually joining X-3 and X-28, and other arrivals from Java, at Broome in the evening.

Four Catalinas of GVT 17, and X-1 and X-20 of GVT 7, landed the next morning, 3 March. Their crews and passengers – including crew members' families – were still on board when nine Zero-sens from Kupang appeared overhead and then commenced a devastating strafing attack. All 15 flying boats in Roebuck Bay, and seven aircraft parked at nearby Broome airfield, were left in flames. Although the Japanese pilots refrained from strafing people in the water, many perished as they swam through burning fuel. The nine Dutch flying boats were carrying an estimated 140 people, of whom 57 were killed. In all, at least 70 people lost their lives in the raid, not counting WO Osamu Kudo, who was shot down by ground fire in his Zero-sen. Among the survivors from the GVT 17 Catalinas were Adm Doorman's wife and their six-year-old son, Theo.

The remaining two Dorniers of GVT 7, X-24 and X-36, escaped the inferno. X-36 ran out of fuel to the west of Broome and stranded at Eighty Mile Beach. Damaged by the reef offshore, the aircraft was then destroyed by its crew. X-24 set down off the same stretch of coast near Wallal sheep station. A short while later an NEI Army L-18 Lodestar landed at the station's airstrip and fuel was siphoned out of its tanks and transferred to X-24 via the flying boat's dinghy. The seaplane reached Broome shortly after the raid, before continuing south to Perth on 7 March.

Whether taken on 2 March 1942 or not, this photograph does convey the scene in Roebuck Bay on the eve of the Japanese attack as the occupants of a Do 24 are ferried ashore. At least 70 people lost their lives when Zero-sens strafed the flying boats moored in the bay and aircraft parked at Broome airfield (*Aviation Heritage Museum of Western Australia*)

This photograph shows X-24 moored in the Swan River near Crawley, Western Australia, having avoided the Broome raid thanks to a navigation error. Note that the new Dutch flag insignia has already been applied to the seaplane. The only surviving cannon turret X-boat, this aircraft was subsequently used for flights into Dutch New Guinea on behalf of the Dutch intelligence service (*Aviation Heritage Museum of Western Australia*)

The five flying school Do 24s despatched earlier (X-5 and X-7 through to X-10) had reached Australia safely, eventually being based at RAAF Rathmines, a seaplane station on Lake Macquarie, north of Sydney. According to Australian flying boat captain Bryan Monkton in his book *The Boats I Flew*, the Dutch 'did not bother to moor up but simply ran them ashore, declaring the war was over and Australia could have their aircraft'. This seems to be a somewhat simplified account, however. At least one Do 24, X-8, had already seen use in a transport role in Australia's top end, making flights between Townsville and Karumba, across the Cape York Peninsula, prior to heading south for Rathmines on 12 April. It got stuck in Gladstone with engine problems, however, and X-10 was used to fly in assistance. X-8 eventually made it to Rathmines on 1 May.

Evidently, the five X-boats were in a poor condition after three months of war, despite them being training aircraft that had not seen prolonged combat. In any case, Dutch flying training was moved to the United States, and the six surviving Do 24s, including X-24, were sold off to the RAAF on 29 April 1942. Due to their poor condition, the purchase price agreed upon was one-sixth that of the original price paid by the Dutch to Dornier. Subsequently, X-24 was exempted from the deal, as the Dutch wanted to retain it for use as a special missions aircraft. After an overhaul at Lake Boga, Victoria, it was returned to the Dutch navy on 8 June.

ON HER MAJESTY'S SECRET SERVICE

X-24 was the only surviving cannon turret X-boat, and it was assigned to the Australia Detachment of the MLD, based at Sydney-Rose Bay. From there it flew missions on behalf of the Netherlands Forces Intelligence Service (NEFIS). The first such flight took place in June 1942 with the aim of contacting Dr Victor de Bruijn, an NEI civil servant who led a small Dutch outpost in New Guinea's Wissel Lakes (now named Paniai Lakes). These highland lakes had only been discovered in 1936 by pilot Frits Wissel. A camp had been

A 'boating atmosphere' surrounds photographs of X-24 in service with the MLD's Australia Detachment. More often than not, '*Ouwe Lobbes*' was unserviceable. Its deplorable condition made its secretive flights into Dutch New Guinea all the more dangerous, however (*P Staal*)

built there two years later, and Dr De Bruijn, who was fascinated with New Guinea and the culture of its Papua peoples, had been flown to the site in a Do 24 in January 1939.

The pilot for the first NEFIS mission was Bastiaan Sjerp, who had sunk the destroyer *Shinonome* and managed to escape from the sinking of the X-20 at Broome along with his wife and one-year-old son. Maj Simon Spoor (who went on to become commander of the NEI Army in 1946) was carried as a passenger. Departing from Sydney on 13 June, they spent a night at Groote Eylandt before flying to Dobo, in the Aru Islands – another unoccupied Dutch outpost. The next day they continued to the Wissel Lakes for a brief meeting with the 'Jungle Pimpernel' ('Jungle Burnet'), as De Bruijn was called, before returning to Australia via Merauke, the main settlement on the south coast of Dutch New Guinea, which also remained in Dutch hands.

A second mission to the camp was flown on 23 July, this time by Lt Will Aernout. He had been tasked with flying Victor de Bruijn to Australia for consultations and medical treatment. The Do 24 ran out of fuel on the way back, however, and the crew made an emergency landing near the coast, 90 miles west of Merauke. After three days fuel was delivered by boat from Merauke, allowing the men to leave their mosquito-infested campsite. The Do 24's R-1820-F52 Cyclone engines had always used more fuel than advertised, but now the fuel consumption of '*Ouwe Lobbes*' (old, friendly big dog), as X-24 was christened, was going through the roof. The Do 24's vice of leaking fuel from its tanks into the sponsons was also a vexing issue for the crew as they navigated the flying boat over some of the world's most inhospitable territory.

Engine problems affected several, if not all, of the X-boat's further missions into New Guinea and to the Aru Islands, and an American PBY had to be borrowed instead. On 2 March 1943 X-24 left Rose Bay, Sydney for a flight to Taneh Merah, formerly a notorious Dutch penal camp on the Upper Digul River. Shortly after takeoff, however, the flying boat made an emergency landing near Taree, in New South Wales, with a cracked cylinder head on its port engine. Clearly '*Ouwe Lobbes*' was no longer fit to fly such missions. In April X-24 was duly replaced by Y-45 – a Dutch Catalina that had been operating from Ceylon with the RAF's No 321 (Dutch) Sqn. X-24 was added to the RAAF's small Do 24 fleet on 8 November 1943, thus ending the X-boats' career in the Royal Netherlands Navy.

CHAPTER FOUR

ATLANTIC COAST RESCUE

By the time the Dutch navy's X-boats were being mauled in Southeast Asia, the Do 24 was established in service with the *Seenotdienst* of the Luftwaffe, although still in limited numbers. About 20 Do 24Ts had been delivered to Germany by Aviolanda during 1941, following the 13 or so Cyclone-powered Do 24Ns – of the latter, more than half had already been lost through operational and non-operational accidents, and enemy action.

As mentioned in Chapter 2, the type had first joined the *Seenotdienst* in July 1940 when two Do 24Ns were sent to Norderney on a trial basis. It was during the same month that the *Seenotdienst* seaplanes, unarmed and painted white with Red Cross markings, were first targeted by the enemy, to the alarm of their crews who had assumed they were flying under the protection of international law. In the run-up to the Battle of Britain, He 59 D-A+SAM became the first to be shot down off Sunderland on 1 July, and five more Heinkel floatplanes were lost to British action before the month was out.

The British suspected that the *Seenotdienst* aircraft were reporting on their shipping. They argued that the Geneva Convention did not cover ambulance aircraft, and that their military potential as aerial observation posts was just too great in a battle zone. The Germans protested, pointing out that the *Seenotdienst* rescued Allied servicemen as well as Germans, which indeed it did. This was not a matter of unqualified charity, however. It is clear that both sides considered the rescue of each other's airmen well worth the trouble simply and coolly for their capture and interrogation.

The first Do 24 loss occurred as early as 17 August 1940. During the previous evening He 59 D-A+FFK was in the process of rescuing a He 111 crew of III./KG 26 from the North Sea when it was attacked on the surface and destroyed by an RAF Coastal Command Hudson (identified as a Blenheim by the Germans). At first light the following day, four more He 59s and Do 24 D-A+PDA took off from Norderney. They found the two surviving crewmen of D-A+FFK clinging to a float from their capsized aeroplane, and the four-man crew of the He 111 in a dinghy nearby. As the wind had increased to a force 6, the He 59s were unable to

At Brest-Poulmic, in Brittany, *Seenotstaffel* 1 enjoyed good facilities constructed for the *Aéronavale*. Note that the Do 24N's outer engines are already running in this photograph (*P Staal*)

land, but Karl Born in the Do 24 attempted his first rough-water landing in the type, only to hit a high wave with such a force that all three engines were torn off. Born and his crew, and the six other survivors, were eventually picked up by a German patrol boat, but both the He 59 and the Do 24 sank to the bottom of the sea.

The losses suffered by the *Seenotdienst* in the early summer of 1940 had prompted the Luftwaffe to issue an order on 29 July instructing that all of its remaining aeroplanes were to be armed and painted as frontline aircraft as soon as possible, given the continuing attacks against them. The rescue service was fully militarised on 25 November 1940, when the *Seenotflugkommandos* were re-designated *Seenotstaffeln* (sea emergency squadrons). Local rescue command posts were known as *Seenotbezirkstellen*, and later as *Seenotkommandos*, with more command units existing at *Luftflotte* (air fleet) level. In a 1944 reorganisation, *Seenotstaffeln* and rescue boat units were grouped in *Seenotgruppen*, which replaced the command posts. Earlier, *Seenotgruppen* had existed as administrative units only. This account will focus on the *Seenotstaffeln*, which, with their *Aussenstellen* (outposts, i.e. detachments) were the actual flying units.

As the war engulfed the whole of Europe, the *Seenotdienst* saw action in virtually all the European seas, the original two squadrons being increased in number to ten by 1942 – the Do 24's exploits in the Mediterranean, the Black Sea and the Baltic will be described in separate chapters. All *Seenotstaffeln* flew the Do 24, although the He 59 soldiered on for a long time and other seaplanes and landplanes were employed too. These included the Fw 58 Weihe light twin, which, equipped with droppable dinghies, was used as a search aircraft both by some of the *Seenotstaffeln* and by frontline units.

It should be kept in mind that the *Seenotdienst* was not exclusively equipped with aircraft – boats continued to play an important role too. Even its aircrew required real seamanship, as well as airmanship. Indeed, the service often felt like a maverick, ill-understood by the Luftwaffe's top brass, and more at home in maritime circles.

SEENOTSTAFFEL 1

The Breguet Bizerte was slow but extremely seaworthy, and visibility from the long greenhouse cockpit was excellent. A total of 21 saw service with the *Seenotdienst* on the shores of France (*T Postma*)

Seenotflugkommando 1, as it then was, sent He 59 flights to Denmark, Norway, Holland and France from Norderney in the spring of 1940, and as more squadrons were created it moved its headquarters to Poulmic, the seaplane base in the harbour of Brest, in July, assuming responsibility for the French Atlantic coast. A detachment was also based at Hourtin, on a coastal lake near Bordeaux. Do 24Ns were assigned to *Seenotstaffel* 1 from the autumn of 1940, KK+UM being the first to arrive at Brest on 22 September. This machine returned to Travemünde in November, however – it seems that some post-production modifications on these aircraft had still to be carried out. When redelivered, most were sent to *Seenotstaffel* 6 in the Mediterranean, which meant that the Do 24Ns did not see a lot of service with 1. *Staffel.* The 14 March 1941 loss of KK+UO, which sunk in the harbour of Brest in a heavy swell while being towed, did not help.

Fortunately for the *Seenotdienst*, the German conquerors had chanced upon a French seaplane that ranked as a good second behind the Do 24 when it came to performing the sea rescue mission. A tri-motor biplane flying boat of Short ancestry, the Breguet 521 Bizerte was liked well enough that an additional eight were bought from the Vichy government to supplement a handful of captured examples. While slow, it was credited with sea state 5 (rough) capability, and according to one experienced *Seenotdienst* pilot, the Bizerte's seaworthiness was actually unmatched by any other aircraft. Six Bizertes were based at Brest and two at Hourtin, and they were joined by a number of Do 24Ts from July 1941.

The Do 24's large radius of action was particularly useful in providing rescue cover for the Luftwaffe's and the Kriegsmarine's Atlantic operations. On 31 January 1942, the German merchantman *Spreewald*, which was returning from the Far East carrying a precious load of rubber, tin, tungsten and quinine, as well as 86 British prisoners taken on board from the auxiliary cruiser *Kormoran*, was accidentally torpedoed by the submarine *U-333* north of the Azores. *U-105* managed to rescue 25 of the 66 crewmen, as well as 55 of the prisoners. On 5 February a Do 24 from Brest was called in to pick up a survivor suffering from blood poisoning while the submarine was heading for Lorient. The aircraft was seriously damaged, however, when landing on the rough sea. The U-boat had to receive the seven crew of the flying boat as well, and then sink the Do 24 with its deck gun.

Within a week of the return of this crew by submarine, a fully blown rescue action was performed even farther out to sea, with Do 24T-1 KK+US saving the crew of an Fw 200C-3 Condor anti-shipping bomber of KG 40. F8+FL had ditched roughly 400 miles to the north-northwest of Cape Finisterre on 13 February. Apparently, the Do 24 *(text continues on page 49)*

34

COLOUR PLATES

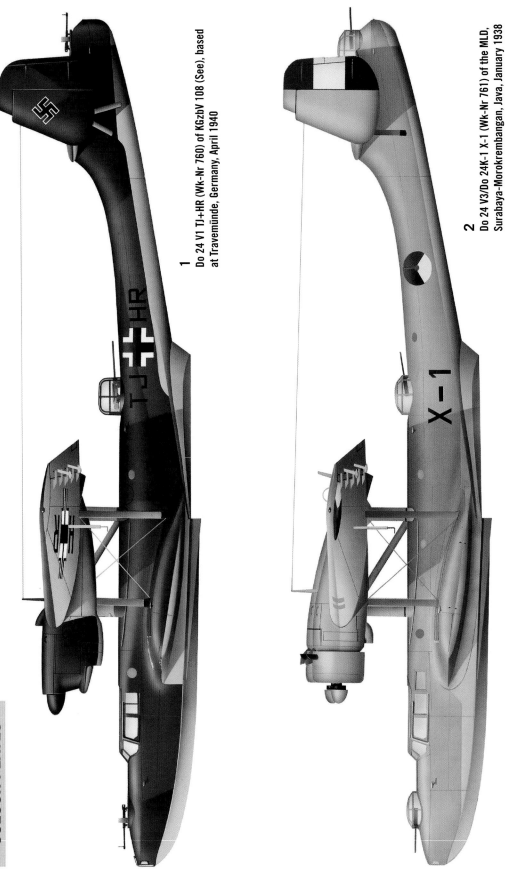

1
Do 24 V1 TJ+HR (Wk-Nr 760) of KGzbV 108 (See), based at Travemünde, Germany, April 1940

2
Do 24 V3/Do 24K-1 X-1 (Wk-Nr 761) of the MLD, Surabaya-Morokrembangan, Java, January 1938

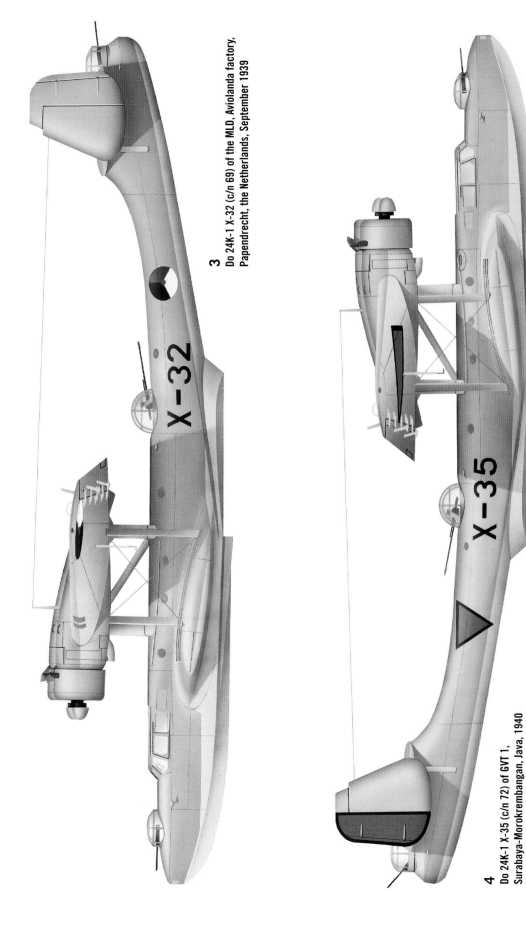

3
Do 24K-1 X-32 (c/n 69) of the MLD, Aviolanda factory,
Papendrecht, the Netherlands, September 1939

4
Do 24K-1 X-35 (c/n 72) of GVT 1,
Surabaya-Morokrembangan, Java, 1940

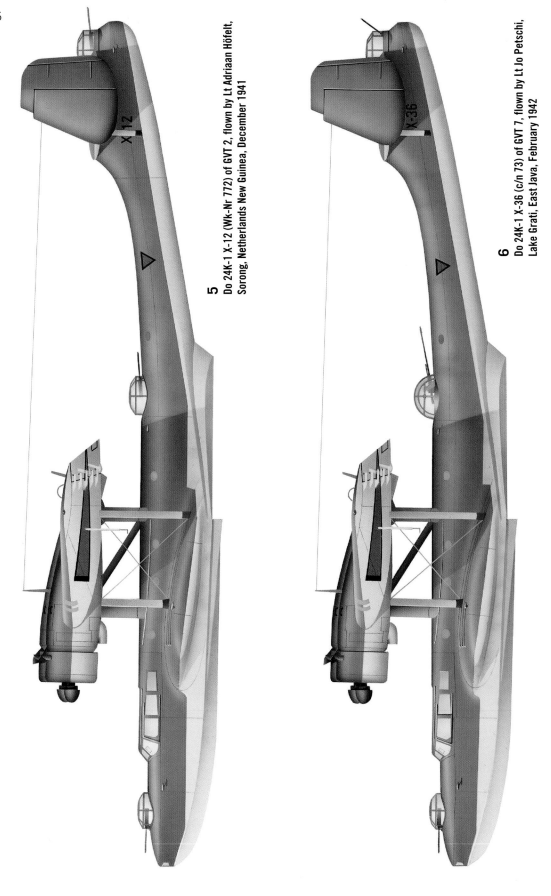

5
Do 24K-1 X-12 (Wk-Nr 772) of GVT 2, flown by Lt Adriaan Höfelt, Sorong, Netherlands New Guinea, December 1941

6
Do 24K-1 X-36 (c/n 73) of GVT 7, flown by Lt Jo Petschi, Lake Grati, East Java, February 1942

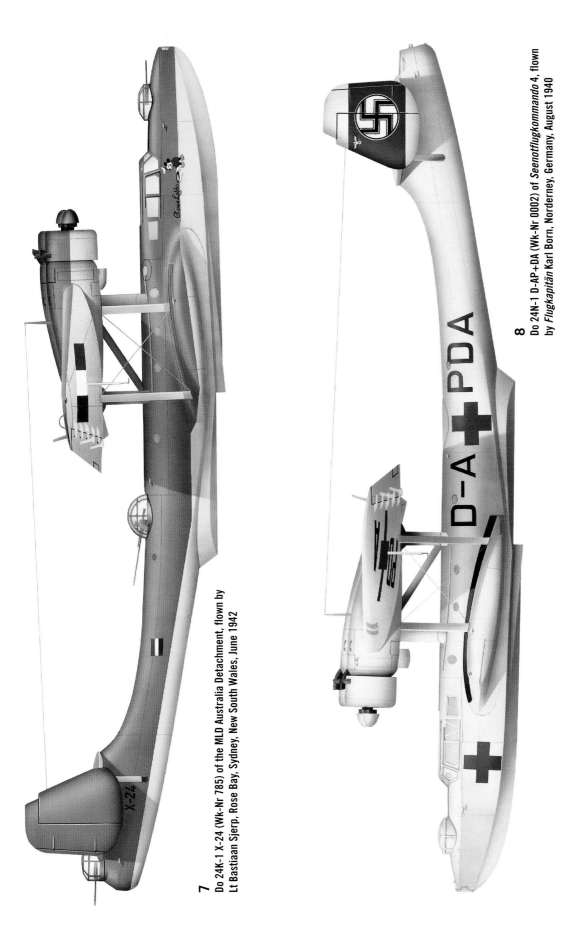

7
Do 24K-1 X-24 (Wk-Nr 785) of the MLD Australia Detachment, flown by
Lt Bastiaan Sjerp, Rose Bay, Sydney, New South Wales, June 1942

8
Do 24N-1 D-AP+DA (Wk-Nr 0002) of *Seenotflugkommando 4*, flown
by *Flugkapitän* Karl Born, Norderney, Germany, August 1940

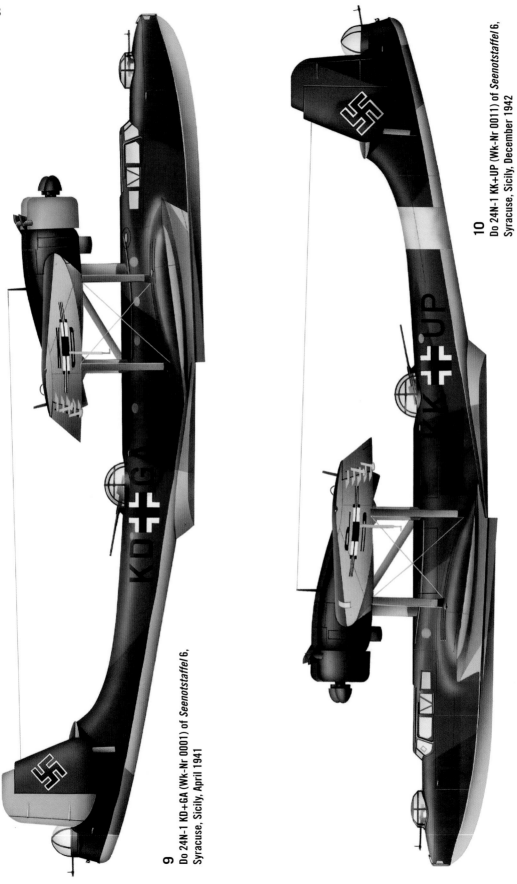

9
Do 24N-1 KD+GA (Wk-Nr 0001) of *Seenotstaffel 6*,
Syracuse, Sicily, April 1941

10
Do 24N-1 KK+UP (Wk-Nr 0011) of *Seenotstaffel 6*,
Syracuse, Sicily, December 1942

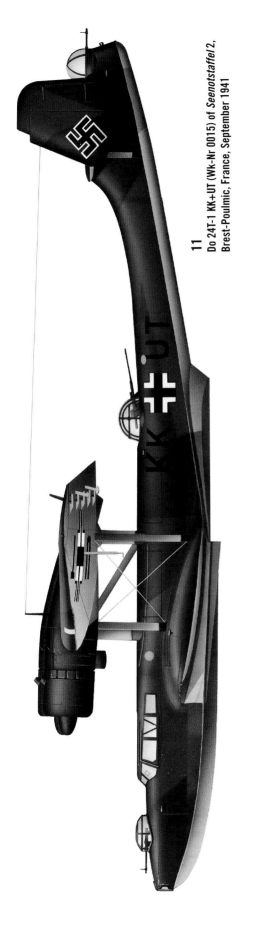

11
Do 24T-1 KK+UT (Wk-Nr 0015) of *Seenotstaffel* 2,
Brest-Poulmic, France, September 1941

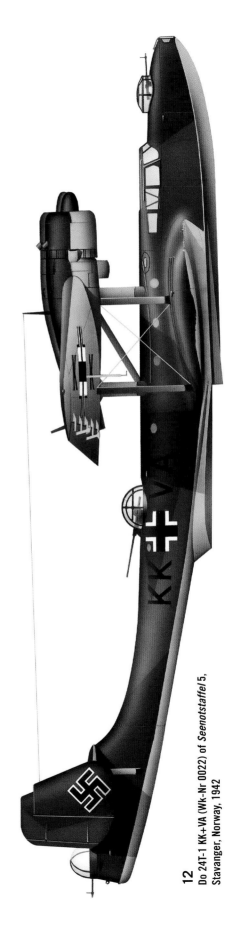

12
Do 24T-1 KK+VA (Wk-Nr 0022) of *Seenotstaffel* 5,
Stavanger, Norway, 1942

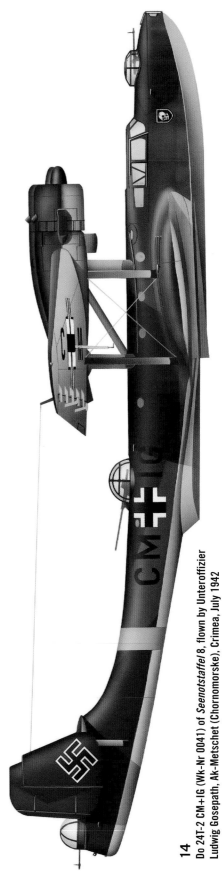

13
Do 24T-2 CM+IS (Wk-Nr 0053) of *Seenotstaffel* 3,
Amsterdam-Schellingwoude, Holland, 1942

14
Do 24T-2 CM+IG (Wk-Nr 0041) of *Seenotstaffel* 8, flown by Unteroffizier
Ludwig Gosepath, Ak-Metschet (Chornomorske), Crimea, July 1942

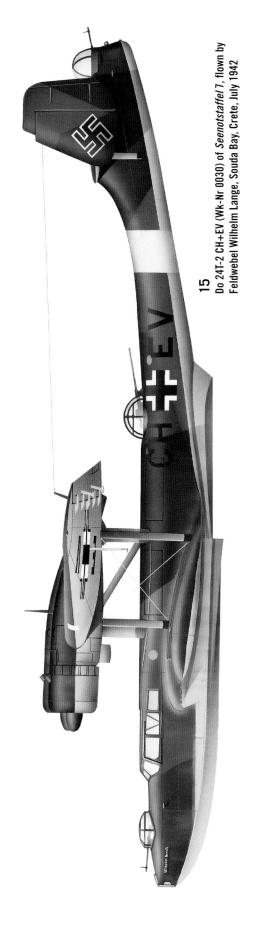

15
Do 24T-2 CH+EV (Wk-Nr 0030) of *Seenotstaffel* 7, flown by
Feldwebel Wilhelm Lange, Souda Bay, Crete, July 1942

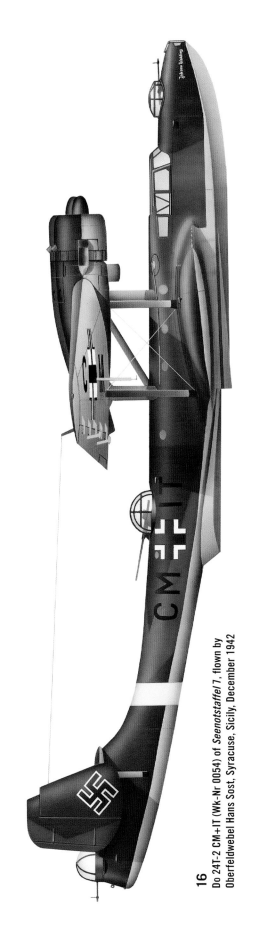

16
Do 24T-2 CM+IT (Wk-Nr 0054) of *Seenotstaffel* 7, flown by
Oberfeldwebel Hans Sost, Syracuse, Sicily, December 1942

42

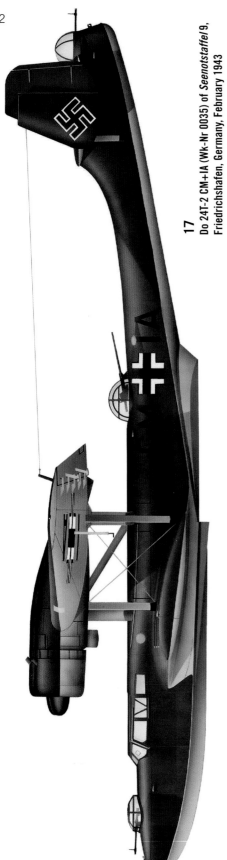

17
Do 24T-2 CM+IA (Wk-Nr 0035) of *Seenotstaffel 9*,
Friedrichshafen, Germany, February 1943

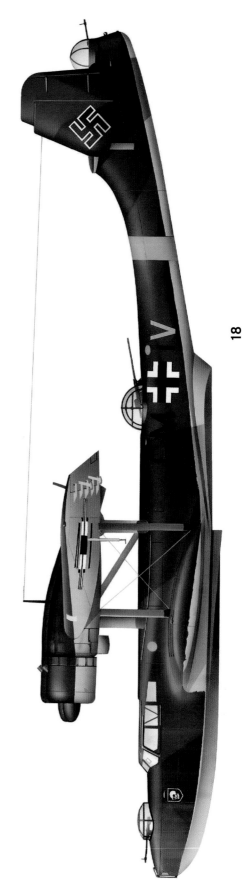

18
Do 24T-2 CM+IV (Wk-Nr 0056) of *Seenotstaffel 8*, flown by Leutnant
Werner Lange, Ortasli-See (Lake Tobechiskoye), Crimea, February 1943

19
Do 24T-2 CH+EX (Wk-Nr 0032) of *Seenotstaffel* 7, flown by Unteroffizier
Hans Lieber, Athens-Phaleron, Greece, October 1943

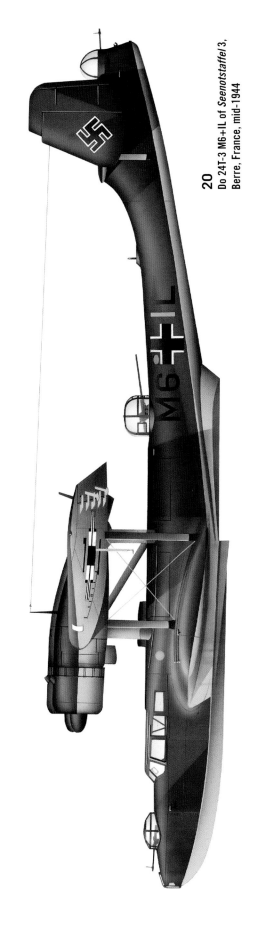

20
Do 24T-3 M6+IL of *Seenotstaffel* 3,
Berre, France, mid-1944

44

21
Do 24T-3 W4+BH (Wk-Nr 1007) of *Seenotstaffel* 1, flown by Feldwebel
Heinrich Reif, Biscarrosse-Hourtiquets, France, August 1944

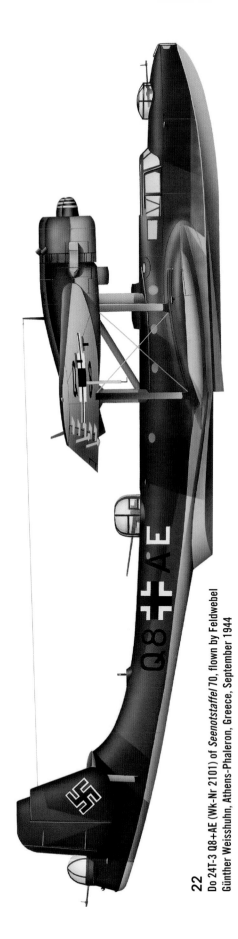

22
Do 24T-3 Q8+AE (Wk-Nr 2101) of *Seenotstaffel* 70, flown by Feldwebel
Günther Weisshuhn, Athens-Phaleron, Greece, September 1944

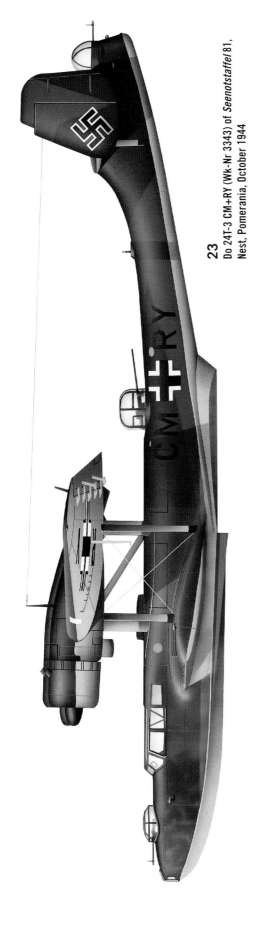

23
Do 24T-3 CM+RY (Wk-Nr 3343) of *Seenotstaffel 81*,
Nest, Pomerania, October 1944

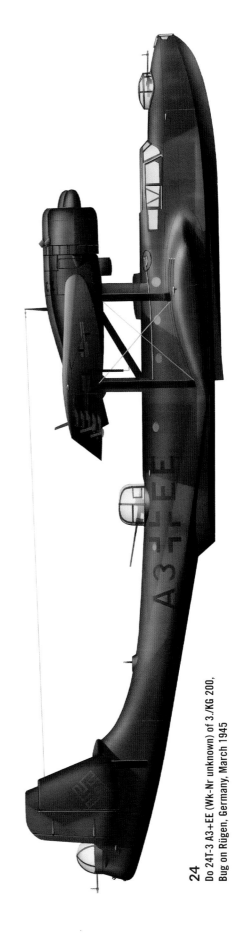

24
Do 24T-3 A3+EE (Wk-Nr unknown) of 3./KG 200,
Bug on Rügen, Germany, March 1945

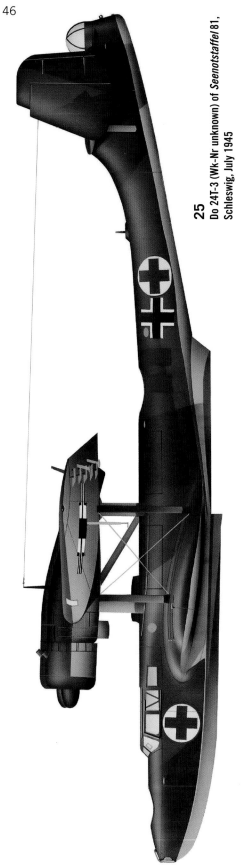

25
Do 24T-3 (Wk-Nr unknown) of *Seenotstaffel* 81,
Schleswig, July 1945

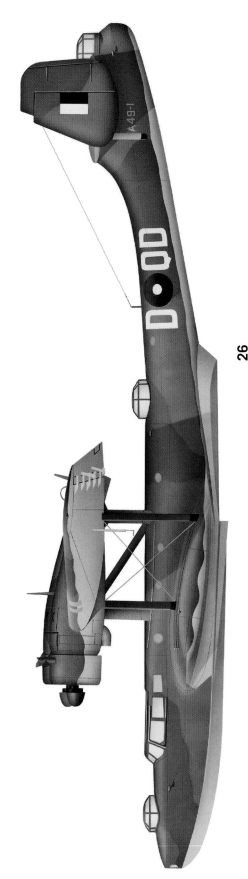

26
Do 24K-1 A49-1/DQ-D (Wk-Nr 765) of No 41 Sqn, RAAF, detached to
No 8 Communications Unit, Kiriwina, Tobriand Islands, March 1944

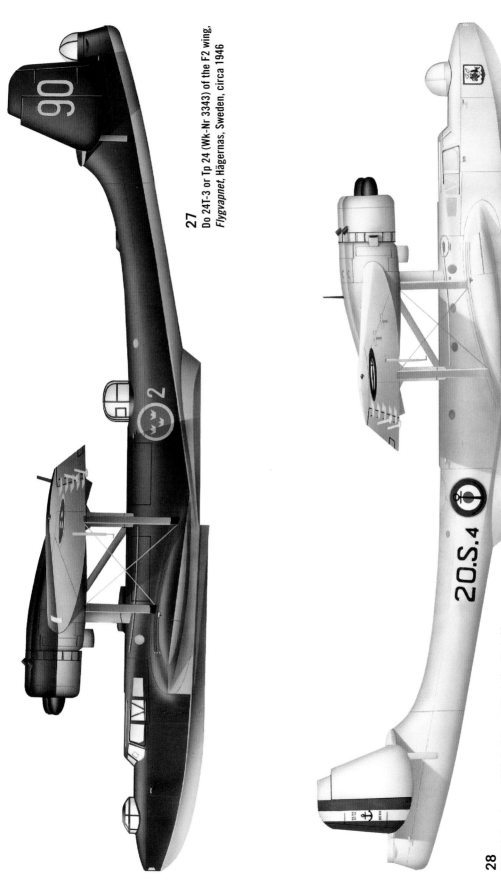

27
Do 24T-3 or Tp 24 (Wk-Nr 3343) of the F2 wing,
Flygvapnet, Hägernäs, Sweden, circa 1946

28
Do 24 (c/n unknown) 20S-4 of *Escadrille de Servitude 20*,
Aéronavale, Ajaccio-Aspretto, Corsica, circa 1949

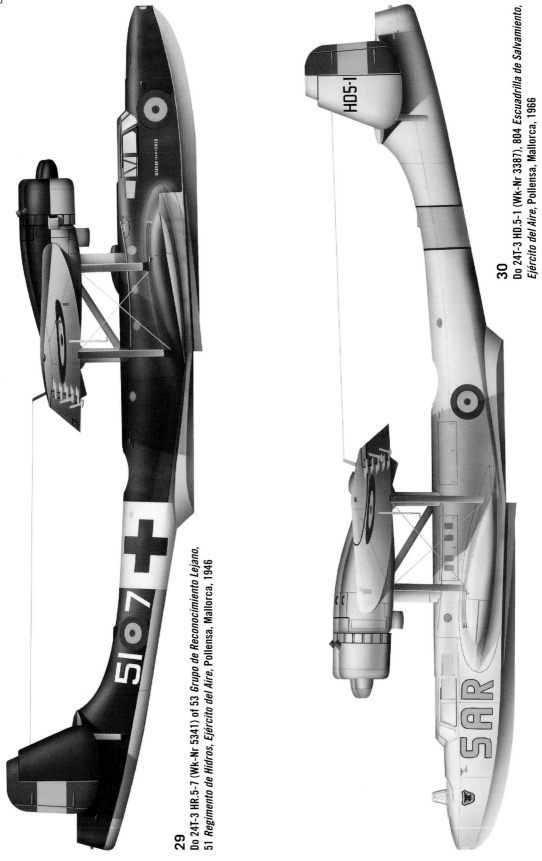

29
Do 24T-3 HR.5-7 (Wk-Nr 5341) of 53 *Grupo de Reconocimiento Lejano,*
51 *Regimento de Hidros, Ejército del Aire,* Pollensa, Mallorca, 1946

30
Do 24T-3 HD.5-1 (Wk-Nr 3387), 804 *Escuadrilla de Salvamiento,*
Ejército del Aire, Pollensa, Mallorca, 1966

During the evening of 8 June 1944, two days after D-Day, part of the crew of the sunken submarine *U-970* was rescued by Do 24 W4+EH. The 14 men had spent 24 hours in a dinghy by the time they were picked up (*T Postma*)

Do 24T-2 CM+IS entered service in May 1942 with *Seenotstaffel* 3. This unit's badge (seen here beneath the cockpit of the seaplane) was a white seagull carrying a red life belt on a pale blue shield. It looks like a propaganda cameraman is filming a staged rescue action in this photograph (*P Staal*)

crew was not sure that they could make it back to France, and on the 15th the flying boat landed in the Ría de Camariñas, on the northwest tip of Spain. The Spanish sent a fuel truck from Rozas airfield, and in spite of protests by the British embassy, the Germans were duly allowed to refuel their seaplane and then leave their peaceful refuge to return to their war.

Squadron codes replaced the *Stammkenzeichen* registration letters on *Seenotstaffeln* aeroplanes in the spring of 1944, the Do 24s and Bizertes of *Seenotstaffel* 1 receiving W4+.H codes. Two Do 24s were destroyed at Brest by an Allied air attack on 8 May 1944, leaving five Do 24s and three Bizertes with the *Staffel* by D-Day.

Of the U-boats ordered to attack the invasion fleet on 6 June 1944, several were sunk, including *U-970*, which was taken out by depth charges dropped from a Sunderland III of No 228 Sqn during the evening of 7 June. Only the bridge and flak crew made it into the dinghies before the vessel sank, and these 14 survivors were rescued in the last light of the following day by Do 24T-3 W4+EH, piloted by Oberfeldwebel Fritz Krummel, which landed safely in Brest at 2327 hrs.

The invasion in Normandy was the beginning of the end for *Seenotstaffel* 1, which, for a brief period, moved south to Biscarrosse-Hourtiquets, a transatlantic seaplane terminal built just before the war. On 12 August orders came to retreat to Germany. During their nocturnal departure on 20 August two Do 24s collided on Lake Biscarrosse. Their crews were taken on board by the remaining flying boats – three Do 24s and two Bizertes. They made for Lake Constance, from where the Do 24s probably flew on to the Baltic theatre.

SEENOTSTAFFEL 2 AND 3

When the *Seenotflugkommandos* were renamed *Seenotstaffeln* in November 1940, two of these units were covering the Channel and the Low Countries coast. Formed in the Baltic, *Seenotstaffel* 2 now found itself based at the French seaplane base of Cherbourg-Querqueville, in Normandy, with

a detachment near Le Havre, on the Seine, at Caudebec. *Seenotstaffel* 3 was based in the port of Boulogne-sur-Mer, although it also used Schellingwoude, an MLD seaplane base to the east of Amsterdam, on the IJsselmeer.

With other theatres receiving higher priority, introduction of the Do 24 here was slow. Indeed, 2. and 3. *Staffel* did not receive their first flying boats until the spring of 1942. Meanwhile, most Luftwaffe fighters had gone east, and the RAF was gaining air superiority over the Dover Strait, prompting 3. *Staffel* to give up Boulogne for the port of Ostend, where a basic seaplane base was built in the Spuikom drainage pool in 1941. Although it was barely large enough for the He 59s to take off from, the pool was more acceptable for the Do 24. Better appointed Schellingwoude was the unit's *de facto* main base, however.

A typical mission here involved the crew of Halifax II W1190 of No 158 Sqn, whose aircraft was damaged by a nightfighter and ditched near the mouth of the Western Scheldt on the night of 1 August 1942. Returning to Amsterdam-Schiphol from a reconnaissance sortie over England, Oberleutnant Gruhle in a Ju 88 of 3.(F)/*Aufkläringsgruppe* 122 sighted a dinghy the following morning. Soon, the seven British airmen, including Sqn Ldr Francis Peter Hewitt, were on board Do 24T CM+IS from Schellingwoude and flown to safety – the safety of a PoW camp, of course.

By then the English Channel was becoming increasingly un-survivable for German seaplanes, and 2. *Staffel* moved its headquarters from Cherbourg to Schellingwoude in late 1942 in order to take over the bases and responsibilities of 3. *Staffel*. The latter had been sent to the French Mediterranean coast. The Channel was now left to the rescue boats.

On 8 October 1943, Do 24T DJ+ZX of 2. *Staffel* was lost 30 miles west of IJmuiden and 65 miles east of Great Yarmouth. There was a British search action going on, too, flown by Anson I EG543 of No 278 Sqn, which was for two American B-24 crew members. Four Spitfire VCs of No 402 Sqn RCAF were to escort the Anson, but they missed the rendezvous and sighted another aircraft instead. The unit's operational record book described the action that ensued in the following entry;

'They recognised this aircraft to be a Do 24. They immediately dropped long-range tanks and attacked. All four pilots gave bursts, and strikes were seen from their fire. The enemy aircraft's port and starboard engines caught fire. It crashed into the sea at a very low height, disappeared and no crew were seen. The aircraft is claimed as destroyed, shared by all four pilots.'

The six crewmen of the Do 24 were never found. While this interception was accidental, by 1944 unescorted rescue flights over the North Sea had become almost suicidal. Few German aircraft still ventured over the North Sea anyway, and in May 1944 *Seenotstaffel* 2 left Amsterdam for the Baltic.

SEENOTSTAFFEL 4 AND 80

As the original squadrons were sent westward in 1940, *Seenotstaffel* 4 took over the *Seenotdienst*'s first base on Norderney. It used seaplane facilities on the islands of Borkum, Langeoog and Sylt too, and was also responsible for a detachment at Aalborg, Jutland, until late 1942. Although Norderney had received the first two Do 24Ns for operational trials, here too the aeroplane was slow to replace the He 59, as 'business' was relatively quiet until late 1942 when Allied strategic bombers started to overfly the German Bight in force and were taken on by Luftwaffe day and nightfighters.

Rescue missions received fighter escorts when they were available, but this was not always the case. On 27 July 1943 at 0436 hrs, Do 24T-3 KO+KB took off from Norderney to search for missing German fighter pilots in an area north of Ameland. There, the flying boat was jumped by Bristol Beaufighter VIF 'V' of No 254 Sqn, flown by Sqn Ldr Filson Young. He later recalled in his combat report;

'Whilst on a shipping reconnaissance over the Dutch coast, Beaufighter V/254 pilot sighted a Dornier 24 slightly above and on the port bow. V/254 increased speed and closed onto the enemy's tail, and opened fire at 450 yards – return fire damaged the port mainplane. The pilot fired a long burst of cannon at 200 yards, using 410 rounds, during which the Do 24 burst into flames and crashed nose first into the sea.'

On 23 August Do 24T-2 CM+IV – which had been transferred from the Black Sea two months earlier – recovered two British airmen from their dinghy in the North Sea. A flight of six B-17s from the USAAF's 303rd Bomb Group (BG) had also been despatched from RAF Molesworth at 1000 hrs to find the two airmen and report their position so that a rescue could be launched. They sighted the empty dinghy at 1357 hrs, and then the Do 24, obviously containing the two Britons, still on the water nearby. Intimidated by the Flying Fortresses, the Germans abandoned the seaplane. The USAAF combat report for the mission read as follows;

'Lt Manning's aircraft – 42-29846 – passed in front of the enemy aircraft and fired several bursts in the water and dropped a smoke bomb. The motors of the enemy aircraft were stopped and it put out what appeared to be three red smoke flares and then put out three yellow dinghies, two of which were lashed together and the other drifted away by itself. At least one man was seen to be in the single dinghy, but no clear observation was made in order to ascertain how many were in the two dinghies that were lashed together.'

One B-17 had climbed to 5000 ft in an attempt to radio a report back to base detailing the position of the flying boat, but this was unsuccessful, and the B-17s headed home – not before destroying the abandoned flying boat, however, as described by 303rd BG historian Gary L Moncur;

'Lt Manning finally came in low over the Do 24 and SSgt H F Jennings, tail gunner, and SSgt R E Montgomery, ball turret gunner, fired 300 to 400 rounds into it, cutting off a part of the tail assembly and starting a fire in one engine. The seaplane burst into flames and was burning profusely when they left the scene. Two crews also reported a second Do 24 or Do 217 [sic] (airborne) in the vicinity of the Do 24 that was on the water. The second aircraft headed for the Dutch coast as soon as the B-17s were sighted.'

Seenotstaffel 4 occupied the cradle of the air-sea rescue service on the German Bight, and the golden tripodal Y shape in its badge – a runic character symbolising life – was associated with the *Seenotdienst* in general. This Do 24 was named after the famous German brandy Asbach Uralt. Its *Stammkennzeichen* is believed to have been KO+JT (*T Postma*)

Both the German and British crews were picked up by the second Do 24 and a rescue boat. Thus the Americans failed to liberate the two Britons, although they were credited with one aircraft destroyed.

To improve the flying boats' chances of survival in such situations, a long-standing wish was fulfilled in the summer of 1944 when a *Such-und-Schutzstaffel* (search and escort squadron) of fighter aircraft was formed under *Seenotdienst* command. Based at Jever, the unit's Me 410s took over the search role, the idea being that they were able to defend themselves and the Do 24s, which now only ventured into the air to perform the actual rescuing of downed airmen.

In August 1944 *Seenotstaffel* 4 was re-designated *Seenotstaffel* 80 as part of *Seenotgruppe* 80, which also included the rescue boats assets of *Seenotflotille* 80. The high level of airmanship and seamanship still present within the *Seenotdienst* was demonstrated when a German patrol boat was hit by bombs near Schiermonnikoog on 26 November. Run aground on the shallows, the VP-Boot broke up, reporting its position to Norderney. Here, a Do 24 was scrambled, its crew led by the *Staffelkapitän*, Oberleutnant Holtkamp. They soon found the stricken vessel, but the low tide only left a narrow, 1600 ft-long gully to land in, in crosswinds and falling darkness. Nevertheless, they managed to rescue all 58 sailors on board – the 13 wounded first, and the others in two more sorties in the dead of night, notwithstanding an attack by an Allied nightfighter during the final takeoff from the gully.

In March 1945 ten Do 24s were flown from Norderney to List, on Sylt, while the *Such-und-Schutzstaffel* moved its nine serviceable Me 410s to Westerland, on the same island. It was from here that *Seenotstaffel* 80 flew its last few operational missions. Shortly before the end of the war, the Do 24s were flown to the Schlei inlet at Schleswig, which was occupied by British troops on 9 May.

SEENOTSTAFFEL 5 AND 10

Sylt was Germany's northernmost island, and almost five years earlier it had become the provisional home base of *Seenotstaffel* 5. This unit was tasked with providing rescue detachments along the extensive Norwegian coastline.

Southeast of the North Cape, near Banak airfield, the Germans constructed a seaplane base in the Billefjord. *Seenotstaffel* 5, and later 10. *Staffel*, maintained a detachment here, at least in the summer months. Two BV 138s can be seen in this photograph, and the rescue Do 24 is lying at the ready, moored to a buoy (*R Albrigtsen*)

The Do 24 could be 'stalled in' to land on the open sea in conditions so rough that, even though the Dornier was a strong aircraft, the whole tail section broke off on a number of occasions. This happened to aircraft CM+IM when coming to the rescue of a He 115 crew off Cape Nordkinn in May 1942. The flightless flying boat limped into Kjøllefjord with the survivors safely on board. Even when still in one piece Do 24s sometimes had to return in boat mode when taking off in heavy seas proved to be an impossible task (*T Postma*)

After the completion of expansion works, the headquarters was moved to the Hafrsfjord at Stavanger, near Sola airfield, in August 1941, with maintenance facilities at Horten, near Oslo. When the Hafrsfjord froze over in winter, Stavanger's seaport had to be used, exposing the aircraft to the elements. The situation was even worse in Bergen, where only one aircraft was usually stationed in the port – wind, fog and downpours often hindered its operations. In Trondheim, the *Seenotdienst* detachment had to compete for facilities with the local *Küstenfliegerstaffel*. Relations with the coastal colleagues were better in Tromsø in the far north, where the *Seenotdienst* opened up shop in October 1941 as the Germans started their attacks on supply convoys sailing between Britain and the Soviet Union.

Around the North Cape, detachments were set up in the Billefjord, where a base for *Küstenflieger* He 115s was built near Banak airfield, and at Kirkenes, in the extreme east of Norway. Drift ice was among the natural hazards here, and aircraft sometimes fell back to Tromsø in winter. The particular benefits of the seaworthy, three-engined, long-legged and well-equipped Do 24 in the Norwegian theatre were obvious, and five examples were already serving with *Seenotstaffel* 5 by late 1941.

In May 1942 convoy PQ 16 was heavily attacked by the Luftwaffe. Whilst on their way home to the Billefjord, two He 115 floatplanes got lost as the city lights of Hammerfest had been switched off by the Kriegsmarine. Running out of fuel, they landed off Cape Nordkinn. Three Do 24s took off, and CM+IM found one crew in a dinghy. Landing in a heavy swell, it was tossed up so violently that the entire rear fuselage was torn off. Fortunately, the rear gunners had left their positions, as prescribed, and closed the rear bulkhead door. The tailless Do 24 was still a boat, and its crew was able to pick up the three survivors and reach the coastal settlement of Kjøllefjord the following day! This was not a unique incident. During the course of the war several Do 24s lost their tail sections in rough open sea landings and managed to limp into port like tailless salamanders.

After PQ 16, of course, came PQ 17, and one of the ships in this infamous convoy was the American steamer *Carlton*, which was torpedoed by *U-88* during the morning of 5 July, sinking within ten minutes. Ten hours later, a Do 24 from Kirkenes landed near the survivors and took 26 of the sailors ashore.

5. *Staffel* took over *Seenotstaffel* 4's detachment at Aalborg in late 1942, before moving it to Kjevik, near Kristiansand, in July 1943. Meanwhile, 5. *Staffel* had been split, the demands of the Arctic theatre meaning that a separate squadron, *Seenotstaffel* 10, was formed at Tromsø in July 1942. The two Norwegian units had 12 Do 24s between them at this time.

On 4 November a damaged Ju 88 of II./KG 30 crash-landed on remote Bear Island (a lone Russian steamer, the *Dekabrist*, was sunk by KG 30 on this date). Rescued by Do 24T-1 KK+UX of 10. *Staffel*, the Ju 88 crew was safely back in Norway before the day was out. Not so lucky were Oberleutnant Rudolf Schütze and his crew, who were intriguingly using an Arado Ar 232 'Millipede' transport aircraft to fly 'Kröte' automatic weather stations to Bear Island and other islands in the Svalbard archipelago. On 26 August 1943 the Ar 232 went missing after taking off from Banak. A search by Do 24 VH+SJ was fruitless, for Schütze had crashed into high ground – there were no survivors.

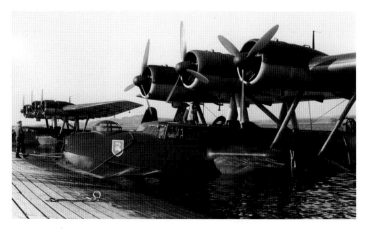

Do 24s at Tromsø in the summer of 1943. The *Seenotstaffel* 10 badge was an elk's head on a dark shield (*P Staal*)

Any flying was hazardous in the Arctic theatre of war, and none more so, perhaps, than rescue flying. Three Do 24s of *Seenotstaffel* 10 were lost with almost all souls on board during the summer of 1943 – one of them, KK+VA, was shot down near Haugesund, in the south of Norway. The aircraft was on loan to the *Führerkurierstaffel* (*Führer's* Courier Squadron) when it was caught by a Mosquito II of the RAF's No 333 (Norwegian) Sqn. It was flying on behalf of the Organisation Todt, which, among other things, was involved in building the Atlantic Wall.

In late September 1943 5. and 10. *Staffel* swapped places to give the latter unit a break. *Seenotstaffel* 10 continued to suffer losses, however, with another of its crews being killed when Do 24T CM+IM was shot down near Frøya by Beaufighter Xs of No 144 Sqn on 14 December and VH+SG having to be written off after a landing accident during a rescue action before the year was out.

SEENOTSTAFFEL 50 AND 51

In August 1944 10. *Staffel*, in the south of Norway, was re-designated *Seenotstaffel* 50, now with its headquarters at Oslo. 5. *Staffel*, in the far north, became *Seenotstaffel* 51 at the same time in a reorganisation designed to save manpower, as more and more men were drafted into combat roles. Young pilot Fritz Reinecke joined the Arctic rescue squadron in 1944, and he later related his experiences in Karl Born's book *Rettung zwischen den Fronten*;

'In 1944, after completing my pilot training and a protracted time with the anti-submarine warfare training squadron [equipped with Do 18s] at Pillau, I volunteered for frontline service and was sent to the *Seenotstaffel* Tromsø. After a few inaugural flights – night and sea landings – I participated in operational sorties. The mission essentially involved the rescue of shot down crews of Ju 88s that had attempted to attack convoys of the Western Allies, loaded with weaponry for the USSR, far north of the North Cape, in the Barents Sea. During the attacks, a Do 24 flew picket in the target area – i.e. we flew to and fro between two map coordinates. During my missions, the weather and swell would not have allowed a landing, however – we could only have dropped dinghies, at least initially. With full tanks and the engines running at economy cruise at a height of 30-160 ft, an endurance of eight hours was possible. After your stint you'd be relieved by another Do 24.

5W+GU of *Seenotstaffel* 50 hanging from a crane somewhere on the Norwegian coast. Note the Arado Ar 196 in the background (*Württembergische Landesbibliothek Stuttgart*)

'On one mission a Do 24 ran out of fuel shortly after its relief. She had to land off the coast and was eventually smashed upon the rocks. The crew got out in a dinghy. On another return flight my crew was spared a similar fate. The flight engineer reported that we only had 200 litres of fuel left – not enough to make it to Tromsø. We managed to land in a quiet fjord southwest of the North Cape and dropped anchor. Bearings were taken from Tromsø to establish our approximate position. A seaplane lighter was to deliver fuel the next morning. Norwegians from a remote little house brought pickled herring out to us in a dinghy, but these weren't needed as we had emergency rations on board, including the stay-awake drug Pervitin.

'The lighter found us the following day and the fuel was transferred to the Do 24 by hand pump for the return flight to Tromsø.

'My very next mission involved the rescue of two meteorologists [from a covert German weather squad] who had drifted off Svalbard in their dinghy in a storm. Apart from not having been called out until two days after this calamity had taken place, we would not have been able to sight anything in the prevailing sea state 7-8, let alone rescue anyone.'

This long, futile mission nearly cost Reinecke and his crew their lives, as on the return leg to Tromsø they entered the wrong fjord and narrowly avoided the cliffs in a climbing 180-degree turn.

U-boats and Ju 88s continued their attacks against the Arctic convoys well into 1945, and Do 24s P7+LN and CM1RJ were lost during rescue actions in the far north on 8 and 21 February, respectively. *Seenotstaffel* 51 ultimately surrendered to the British at Tromsø and Bodø on 8 May 1945. In the south, rescue flying had become almost impossible in the face of Allied air superiority, and three BV 138 flying boats had been assigned to *Seenotstaffel* 50 with the sole task of eavesdropping on Allied fighter communications when the Do 24s were aloft. In the final days of the war at least one Do 24 flew into the Baltic to take part in the evacuation of the Soviet-besieged Courland peninsula.

CHAPTER FIVE

MEDITERRANEAN AND BLACK SEA OPERATIONS

efore turning against the Soviet Union, Hitler had decided, in December 1940, to intervene in the Mediterranean to prevent a complete Italian defeat in Mussolini's campaigns in North Africa and Greece, and to keep the British at bay. The *Seenotdienst* had, by then, proven its value to the German war effort, and thus three southern *Seenotstaffeln* were formed to safeguard the upcoming operations. They were 6. *Staffel*, which was sent to Sicily, 7. *Staffel*, which went to Greece, and 8. *Staffel*, based on the Black Sea coast in Rumania for Operation *Barbarossa*. In addition, *Seenotstaffel* 3 had moved from Holland to the French Mediterranean coast by 1943.

The Mediterranean proved to be no quiet backwater, and although higher sea temperatures increased a downed airman's chances of survival, there was no guarantee he would be rescued due to the heavy swells that were commonplace in-theatre. Such conditions could prevent a Do 24 from landing, or greatly risk the safety of the seaplane and its crew if they attempted to alight. The same was true for the Black Sea, which, despite its resorts, can also experience serious winter weather.

Formerly D-A+EAV and painted in a Red Cross livery, the first *Seenotdienst* Do 24 became KD+GA, and like many of the Cyclone-powered Do 24Ns that had not already been lost, was assigned to *Seenotstaffel* 6 in Syracuse, Sicily in February 1941. It is seen here wearing yellow Balkan campaign paint on the rudders and engine cowlings, although 6. *Staffel* was mainly concerned with supporting the war in North Africa. An unserviceable KD+GA was eventually blown up by retreating German troops in the Gulf of Bumba near Tobruk in November 1941 (*P Staal*)

SEENOTSTAFFEL 6

While old Savoia-Marchetti S.66 'catamaran' flying boats equipped an Italian air-sea rescue unit at Cagliari–Elmas, on Sardinia, the Luftwaffe

Do 24s of 6. *Staffel* at their base on the south side of Syracuse, on the Porto Grande. An Italian Cant Z.506 floatplane can also be seen moored behind the German seaplanes (*P Staal*)

chose not to rely on its allies when it came to retrieving ditched airmen. Instead, it sent *Seenotstaffel* 6 (which had been formed at Kiel-Holtenau) to Syracuse, on Sicily, in February 1941, hard on the heels of the first Luftwaffe units to arrive in-theatre. 6. *Staffel* was initially equipped with nine He 59s and Cyclone-powered Do 24Ns. Besides Syracuse, Italian seaplane bases at Marsala and Cagliari were also used, and by April three He 59s were based on the African coast at Tripoli, in Libya. Detachments at Benghazi and Derna followed as Rommel's *Afrika Korps* advanced. During the Siege of Tobruk, several Do 24s were also stationed in a small port in the Gulf of Bumba.

In June 1941 a Do 24 showed its capabilities by rescuing three Britons from their dinghy in sea state 5 halfway between Tobruk and Crete. A British 'twin-engined seaplane' had been unable to land, and it accompanied the German flying boat for a while in a show of appreciation. There was mutual waving when each seaplane went its own way back to base.

Rommel's first retreat in December 1941 found KD+GA (the first Do 24N tested at Norderney the previous year) unserviceable in the small port in the Gulf of Bumba, and the seaplane had to be destroyed so as to prevent it from falling into Allied hands.

Six months later Tobruk had been taken by the Germans, and on 10 July 1942 a flightless Do 24 limped into the Libyan port with a broken wing strut after a rough landing at sea, some 30 miles out. On board was the Australian crew of Hudson FH300, which had accidentally attacked the German destroyer *Hermes* (a former Greek ship) rather than a merchantman, and duly been shot down by it.

Not only Allied lives were saved by *Seenotstaffel* 6, of course. Among the German pilots rescued during the Siege of Malta in 1942 were two 'big fishes' of *Jagdgeschwader* 53 'Pik As'. The *Geschwaderkommodore*, Major Günther 'Henri' von Maltzahn, was shot down by fighters near Valletta on 11 May while flying a Bf 109F. He was picked up by a Do 24 that evening, and survived the war with 67 victories to his name. Von Maltzahn's *Gruppenkommandeur* in II./JG 53, Hauptmann Gerhard Michalski, was also rescued by a Do 24, having been shot down in his Bf 109G off Marsaxlokk Bay by Spitfires of No 126 Sqn on 15 October. The leading German ace over Malta, Michalski was again caught by Spitfires and rescued for a second time by the *Seenotdienst* on 18 June 1943. He ended the war with 68 kills.

On 1 May 1942 Do 24T-2 CH+EZ, under the command of Paul Metges, was wrecked during a rough landing off Vittoria, Sicily, while attempting to save the life of another JG 53 pilot. The Do 24 pilot, Feldwebel Karl Reinhold, was killed. According to Reinhold's son, a violent wave tore off the centre engine, which then smashed his father's cockpit. Commanded by Leutnant Ernst Warganz, Do 24 KK+UP came to the rescue and

A 6. *Staffel* crew idly watch the tide go by, probably at Syracuse. The intense combat around Malta did keep the squadron busy, however. Although only 13 Cyclone-powered Do 24Ns are thought to have been built for the *Seenotdienst*, *Stammkennzeichen* KD+BH is unaccounted for in the records (*P Staal*)

managed to land in the heavy swell, despite red flares fired by Metges' crew to advise against this. KK+UP was unable to take off again, but with the aid of a patrol boat, KK+UP and all the surviving airmen made it back to base. A similar incident happened on 17 May when CM+IB picked up the crew of Do 24T CM+IN, which had been shot down near Malta. A seaplane support boat attempted to salvage CM+IN, but the burning seaplane eventually sank.

Following the Allied landings in Algeria on 8 November 1942, the Germans moved quickly to secure defensive positions in Tunisia, allowing Rommel's troops to retreat there from El Alamein, in Egypt. Some transport flights into Tunisia – in particular, the Vichy French naval port of Bizerte – were carried out by 6. *Staffel*. A *Seenotdienst* command post was set up in Tunis, and Do 24 CM+IR is known to have been based at Pantelleria (the Italian island close to the Tunisian coast) in early 1943.

On 13 November 1942 the *Staffelkapitän*, Oberleutnant Fritz Wölke, and his crew were killed on a return flight from Tunis when their Do 24 was attacked by a Beaufighter VIC of No 227 Sqn RAF, which also claimed several Ju 52/3ms and SM.82 transports destroyed. The next day another Do 24N was apparently lost on a rescue mission, KK+UP being shot down by Flt Lt Eric Norman in a No 72 Sqn Spitfire VC off Marsaxlokk Bay. Even minelaying in the Strait of Sicily took its toll on 6. *Staffel* as Do 24T-3 VH+SC was blown up while landing off Sicily on 29 December, killing one crewman. To make matters worse, Do 24T-2 CM+IT hit a ship's mast while taking off from Syracuse, bound for North Africa with a cargo of fuel, on 17 December. This aircraft was on loan from 7. *Seenotstaffel*. Oberleutnant Hans Kurz, Oberfeldwebel Hans Sost and their entire crew were killed.

Like its sister squadrons, 6. *Seenotstaffel*, despite its losses, and an increasingly critical situation in Tunisia, was ordered to send two Do 24s to the Black Sea in February 1943 to participate in the Kuban airlift. At the same time the German high command kept pouring reinforcements into Tunisia, despite the havoc wreaked by Allied forces on Axis shipping and transport aircraft – 15 supply vessels and scores of transport aircraft were lost in April alone, including 24 Ju 52/3ms shot down on the 18th. Two days earlier, Do 24T-3 DJ+ZB was downed by P-38 Lightnings off Sciacca, Sicily. Two members of the crew were killed, and they went down with the Do 24. The remaining four were rescued by Italian fishermen, who were less than friendly and demanded the Germans' watches in return for their services.

Hard-pressed 6. *Staffel* got help from their 7. *Seenotstaffel* colleagues in Athens, its CM+IT *Johann Wehling* being seen here at Syracuse in September 1942. The seaplane's crew was led by Oberleutnant Hans Kurz, with Oberfeldwebel Hans Sost being the pilot. They were killed on 17 December when CM+IT hit a ship's mast while taking off from Syracuse harbour, bound for North Africa with a cargo of fuel (*H Thürling*)

A complete formation of 14 six-engined Me 323s, each carrying 12 tonnes of fuel or ammunition, was wiped out off Cape Bon on 22 April. The only rescue action undertaken from the air was by Fieseler Storchs dropping one-man dinghies, and questions were asked about the absence of the *Seenotdienst* (*Luft*). To be fair, the weather was rainy with heavy seas that day. Nevertheless, the exploits of the battered 6. *Staffel* seem to have been somewhat limited in the weeks preceding the Axis surrender in North Africa, which occurred on 13 May. Do 24T-3 DM+RA is known to have been shot down by nightfighters over the Strait of Sicily on 4 May while on a nocturnal transport mission – its crew was killed. On 14 May the *Staffel* suffered another loss when Do 24T-3 DM+RB was shot down by RAF fighters off Sardinia, killing the crew, including Oberleutnant Ernst Warganz, who had taken over from Wölke as *Staffelkapitän*. Do 24T-3 DJ+ZC was also lost off the Sardinian coast on 29 June, but its crew was able to swim to the shore.

Sicily now came under Allied attack, and the invasion of that island and the ensuing surrender of Italy forced the *Staffel* on the move, to Taranto, Vigna di Valle (near Rome), Portofino, La Spezia-Cadimare and, finally, to German-occupied Venice in October, confining the *Staffel* to the Adriatic Sea. Following the Italian surrender, Tito's Partisans took control of the Croatian coast, but the Germans fought back and occupied the city of Split. On 1 November three Do 24s were lost during a supply mission to Split when the city's harbour came under attack from 36 RAF fighter-bombers. Do 24s CM+IE and CM+IJ were shot down, while KK+LQ was destroyed in the port. Flown by Unteroffizier Paul Lösing, CM+IE had just taken off for Venice carrying 16 wounded and a nurse. No one survived.

Some captured Cant Z.506 tri-motor floatplanes were pressed into service by *Seenotstaffel* 6, which also acquired three Fw 190s for search and escort duties. These fighters could not prevent the loss of several Do 24s in Venice due to ground attacks by P-38 Lightnings in March. 6. *Staffel* was finally disbanded on 22 September 1944 when its remaining Dorniers were sent to the Aegean. The Fw 190 flight was renamed *Seenotstaffel* 20, working in concert with rescue boats until February 1945.

SEENOTSTAFFEL 3

The Allied landings in Algeria caused the Germans to occupy Vichy France, as they would now need to defend the French south coast. To cover subsequent operations here, *Seenotstaffel* 3 had transferred from Amsterdam to the seaplane base on the Étang de Berre, near Marseilles, by January 1943. The *Staffel* still had He 59s as well as Do 24s at this time, and two of the biplanes equipped a detachment at St-Raphaël, near

Cannes. Eleven 'new' Breguet Bizertes were captured in Vichy territory and added to the *Seenotdienst* fleet.

While there were probably worse postings than the Côte d'Azur, there was no shortage of dangerous rescue actions here. In July and August 1943, German troops were airlifted into Corsica to replace the Italians, and despite standing patrols mounted by the Do 24s, many ditchings by Ju 52/3m and Me 363 Gigant transports resulted in large losses of life since no life vests or dinghies were provided to passengers on board these aircraft.

The Armistice of Cassibile also meant the surrender of the Italian fleet to the Allies. During the morning of 9 September, three battleships, three cruisers and eight destroyers left La Spezia, but that afternoon the Germans attacked, sinking the battleship *Roma* with Fritz X guided missiles launched by Do 217s from III./KG 100. Of some 1850 souls on board, 1250 were burnt alive or drowned. Two destroyers were also sunk. The next morning, the *Seenotdienst* turned out in force, and several Do 24s landed to start picking up the survivors. One flying boat returned to base with 19 Italian sailors on board. At this point, however, a B-24D Liberator of the USAAF's 1st Antisubmarine Squadron arrived on the scene. Whilst on a patrol mission from its base at Protville 1, in Tunisia, its crew sighted three seaplanes on the water, which were thought to be PBYs at first. The debriefing report continues;

M6+FL (RJ+VY), a French-built Do 24T-3, is hoisted into the Étang de Berre, near Marseilles. Do 24 crews included two mechanics/gunners, and they can be seen here standing on the wing ready to release the crane hook. The remaining four members of the crew – pilot, observer/aircraft commander, radio operator and tail gunner/medic – are standing in the cockpit or sit atop the front turret (*T Postma*)

'Crew sighted a few miles away about 200 survivors in life vests in the water, in lifeboats, in wreckage and on orange and black life rafts. These were strung out about five miles. Aircraft "C" circled and dropped smoke flares when a very large oil slick a few miles long was observed another mile away. After a look at the oil slick Captain decided to return and identify three aircraft. Aircraft "C" passed three-quarters of a mile astern the formation and saw black swastikas on tails, black crosses on wings and fuselage against grey background. Two were Do 24s and one Do 26 [sic] flying boats. Aircraft "C" climbed from 500 ft to 1000 ft and decided to attack with gunfire.

'At this time all three enemy aircraft started taxiing, turning to port to take off. The run-in was made at 50 ft, the attack from starboard of the nearest ship. An S-turn was accomplished in order to attack the other two aircraft on the same run. Bombardier and navigator from the nose, top turret and both waist gunners and tail gunner all fired 0.50-cals when in position. Three more attacks were completed, by which time large flames and smoke were pouring from all three aircraft. Fire, estimated to be 20 mm, was seen coming from nose and top turrets of enemy aircraft. No injury or damage to Aircraft "C", which set course to base due to depletion of ammunition and tail gun being unserviceable.'

German sources claim *four* Do 24s were destroyed by the B-24, adding that all 24 crew members and 69 Italians from them were picked up by

The crew of M6+IL on alert duty, wearing non-inflatable kapok life jackets (*P Staal*)

Pilot Oberleutnant Kurt Wachsmuth commanded *Seenotstaffel 7* during its first operations in Greece. He was transferred elsewhere in February 1942, being succeeded by Oberleutnant Hans Tretter (*H Thürling*)

a rescue boat. American gunfire also killed some 80 Italian sailors, after German bombs had failed to do so.

Wishing to hive off non-combat tasks, the Luftwaffe talked to the Spanish who agreed to set up a neutral rescue squadron for the Western Mediterranean in the Baleares, to be equipped with Do 24s (see Chapter 7). Surprisingly, conversion training of the first Spanish crews took place at Berre. *Seenotstaffel* 3 reported a strength of seven Do 24s, two Bizertes and nine crews on 8 August 1944. The Allied invasion of southern France expedited the end of *Seenotstaffel* 3, the evacuation of the Étang de Berre base starting on 15 August – the day of the Allied landings. Twenty-four hours later the unit reported that three Do 24s were at Lyon and two Do 24s and a Bizerte were already at Friedrichshafen. Soon thereafter 3. *Staffel* was disbanded.

SEENOTSTAFFEL 7

Seenotstaffel 7 was formed to support the Wehrmacht's Greek campaign in the spring of 1941. Five He 59 floatplanes crossed the continent from Amsterdam by way of 'puddle-hopping', with several fuel stops on lakes, on the Danube and at Varna, arriving at Salonica on 22 April. Soon the squadron was involved not only in search and rescue actions, but also in liaison, transport and ambulance flights and dinghy dropping for tactical use.

By early May the conquest of the Greek mainland was complete, and Phaleron Bay, near Athens, became the *Staffel*'s main base. Three Do 24s were transferred here from Sicily. Some Heinkel He 60s had also been sent to Greece, and these elderly reconnaissance floatplanes were employed in the search role on behalf of *Seenotstaffel* 7 as it braced itself for the invasion of Crete, carried out by airborne troops in Ju 52/3ms and reinforcements in flotillas of *caiques*, or wooden fishing boats. The latter were heavily attacked by Royal Navy warships, which in turn were bombed by the Luftwaffe. The emergency centre at Phaleron was flooded with distress calls on 22 May, and the Do 24s flew to and fro to rescue some 175 German soldiers in heavy seas, including 57 in three consecutive sorties by one of the aircraft. Boats impressed by the *Seenotdienst* picked up a further 84 men, including 65 British sailors from the cruiser *Gloucester*, which was sunk by Stukas.

With Crete in German hands, a detachment was based at Souda Bay, allowing coverage of much of the Eastern Mediterranean, and relieving *Seenotstaffel* 6, which was very busy around Malta. *Seenotstaffel* 7 also took over its sister squadron's *Aussenstelle* (detachment) in the Gulf of Bumba, west of Tobruk. Do 24N KK+UO, which had arrived in Athens on 16 July, was sent there 12 days later, and it rescued a He 111 crew on 10 August – the aircraft was piloted by Feldwebel Helmut Steckel throughout this period.

Operating from Souda Bay on 22 February 1942, the crew of Feldwebel Wilhelm Lange in Do 24T-2 CH+EV rescued airmen from another He 111 south of Rhodes. On 12 March, two British airmen were rescued from their dinghy by the Do 24 crew of pilot Feldwebel Hans Sost and observer Oberfeldwebel Richard Marquardt. The next day, the action was re-enacted for a *Deutsche Wochenschau* propaganda newsreel, with the most English-looking *Staffel* members impersonating the survivors.

Two British airmen were rescued by a 7. *Staffel* Do 24 in March 1942, and some of the personnel involved in the mission can be seen in this photograph. They are, from left to right, the pilot, Oberfeldwebel Hans Sost, the observer/aircraft commander, Oberfeldwebel Richard Marquardt, the two Britons (or possibly their German impersonators, as the action was restaged for a propaganda newsreel) and the two mechanics/gunners, Unteroffizier Meyer and Obergefreiter Wallfraff (*H Thürling*)

Damaged in air combat, Do 24T-2 CM+IF crashed during a night landing at Phaleron Bay on 11 April, killing the pilot, Feldwebel August Franke. This Do 24 had only arrived with the *Staffel* on 31 March. The wreck was salvaged the next day, shipped off and apparently rebuilt as a Do 24T-3.

Heavy fighting surrounded Allied convoy MW 11 as it tried to reach Malta from Egypt in June 1942, and *Seenotstaffel* 7 saw a lot of action. Oberfeldwebel Hans Sost and his crew in Do 24T-2 CM+IO fruitlessly searched for a U-boat crew in the early hours of the 14th. Later that day a Ju 88A of 2./LG, flown by the unit's *Staffelkapitän*, Oberleutnant Gerhard Brenner, was shot down in an attack on the convoy. His squadron shadowed the crew's dinghy for several days, but the Do 24s pilots judged a landing in the heavy seas to be too dangerous – justifiably so, as Sost demonstrated when he did land to pick up Bf 109 pilot Leutnant Heinrich Hesse of 7./JG 53 during the afternoon of the 15th. As Sost took off again, CM+IO was lifted up by a big wave and smashed onto the water surface, losing its tail and part of its left wing. The wrecked flying boat stayed afloat, and later that night the crew and the rescued fighter pilot were picked up by the submarine *U-83*, which sank the Dornier with its deck gun and put the airmen ashore at Messina on the 18th.

The crew of CH+EW, which had also crashed, emerged from another U-boat, and the two Do 24 crews were flown back to Souda Bay from Taranto in a BV 222 flying boat on the 21st. Meanwhile, by 17 June, the sea had calmed down, but all the remaining aircraft of the *Aussenstelle* Souda Bay had been damaged, and Leutnant Karl-Heinz Daehn boarded the Italian torpedo boat *Lupo* to mount a final, unsuccessful, search for Oberleutant Brenner's Ju 88 crew.

During the battles of El Alamein, flights into Mersa Matruh were carried out by the Do 24s from Crete. CM+IK was sunk in an Allied air raid against the port on 1 July 1942, and CH+EV was written off there when it was caught in a naval bombardment. Two days earlier, the same aircraft had rescued the three-man crew of a Ju 88C nightfighter of 1./NJG 2 some 19 miles to the south of Crete.

On 29 August a Junkers Ju 86 reconnaissance aircraft of 2(F)./123, based at Kastelli on Crete, photographed the Suez Canal from an altitude of 33,000 ft – the high-flying Ju 86 was a more successful application

Whilst moored at Mersa Matruh, in Egypt, CH+EV was damaged in a naval bombardment on 12 July 1942, and subsequently abandoned. *Wilhelm Arndt* had been used to rescue a Ju 88C nightfighter crew off Crete 48 hours earlier (*P Staal*)

Leutnant Karl-Heinz Daehn and Oberfeldwebel Marquardt in the situation room. Daehn became 7. *Staffel's* last commander in 1944, while Richard Marquardt was killed in action on 23 December 1943. Immediately above Marquardt's head on the large-scale map is the Crimea. Frequent transfers took place between the Aegean and Black Sea theatres, with the Do 24s overflying Bulgaria to avoid Turkish territory (*H Thürling*)

of the Jumo diesel engine. On its way home, however, one Jumo gave up and the aircraft ditched in the Mediterranean. The rescue by a Do 24 was uneventful, except that the *Seenotstaffel* 7 crew did not quite believe the pilot and his observer when they stated that there were only two souls on board! Events in September included the rescue of a four-man Ju 88 crew on the 7th and of a six-man He 111 crew on the 30th.

Early in the morning of 12 October a rescue action near the island of Gavdos was also successful thanks to the help of a Beaufighter pilot who buzzed the Do 24T-2 CM+IX of Oberfeldwebel Wilhelm Sommer and Leutnant Karl-Heinz Daehn. At first the Germans thought they were being attacked, but then the Beaufighter waggled its wings and pointed them towards the dinghy they were searching for, containing four Britons who received treatment on board on the way back to Souda Bay. The same crew took off for another mission at 1030 hrs to pick up nine wounded crew members of a damaged Italian torpedo boat to the south of Crete.

The parlous state of Rommel's supply chain on the eve of the Second Battle of El Alamein meant that CM+IX was forced to undertake transport flights into Tobruk from 18-20 October, carrying petrol for the local *Seenotdienst* boat. While at Tobruk on the 20th, pilot Obergefreiter Wilhelm Ritzrau and his crew were scrambled on a sea rescue off Alamein, but they only found an empty dinghy before landing at Mersa Matruh. During the battle, still flying CM+IX out of Souda Bay, Ritzrau's crew rescued three British airmen on 2 November and flew five fruitless rescue missions from 5-8 November. CM+IX ultimately crashed off Antikythera on 24 May 1943 after a fire had broken out during a flight. Four of its crew were killed, but pilot Oberfeldwebel Willi Gebhardt and the tail gunner survived.

1943 was only two days old when ten men were rescued by Do 24T-2 CH+EX from Phaleron, the seaplane being flown by the *Staffelkapitän*, Oberleutnant Hans Tretter. Promoted to Hauptmann, Tretter flew to the Crimea in Do 24T-3 DJ+ZM in late February to command the Do 24 component of the Kuban airlift. He returned to Athens on 3 April.

Much of Greece was under Italian occupation, but following Italy's surrender on 8 September 1943, German troops were duly despatched to take over their positions. Fighting broke out in some places, notably in Cephalonia, where thousands of Italian soldiers were eventually executed by the Germans, and in the Dodecanese after the landing of British forces. Unsurprisingly, *Seenotstaffel* 7 was kept busy flying rescue and transport operations.

On 15 September Ju 87Ds of *Stukageschwader* (StG) 3 started bombing the Italian garrison on Cephalonia, and on the 16th a Stuka ditched to the west of the island due to engine trouble. At 0720 hrs the next morning KO+KA took off from Phaleron Bay. Pilot Oberfeldwebel Friedrich Becker landed alongside the surviving airmen in sea state 1, and the Do 24T-3 returned to Athens at 1015 hrs. Later that day the same crew flew another rescue mission, returning after dark at 2010 hrs. With the base blacked out due to the presence of enemy aircraft in the area, Becker crashed his aircraft into a quay wall, resulting in serious injury to the crew and heavy damage to the flying boat.

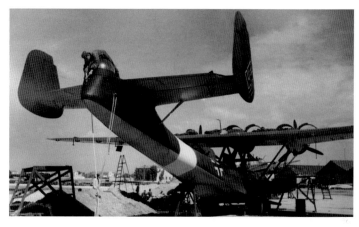

For proper maintenance, the ability to pull or hoist the flying boats ashore was important, and a crane was installed at Athens-Phaleron by the Germans for this very purpose. However, one cannot help thinking that work on the Do 24's upswept tail was better done on the water (*P Staal*)

On 8 October the steamer *Ingeborg*, which had left Piraeus carrying troops of a penal battalion, was attacked by British aircraft. Replacements for wounded sailors were brought on board by a Do 24, and the ship put in at Syros. The journey was subsequently continued, but on the 29th *Ingeborg* was torpedoed by the British submarine HMS *Unsparing* near Amorgos. A total of 52 survivors were rescued by three Do 24s. Meanwhile, on the 16th, the freighter *Kari*, carrying 500 German troops, had been sunk by the Royal Navy submarine HMS *Torbay* in the same area. Do 24T-3 VH+SK scrambled and picked up 18 men, only to crash during takeoff due to an engine failure. Survivors were rescued by the Kriegsmarine vessel *UJ-2110*.

One Do 24 under Karl-Heinz Daehn was sent west to Durazzo (Durrës) on 12 October to reconnoitre the situation along the Italian-occupied Adriatic coast. Shot at several times by Italian forces, the seaplane safely returned to Athens on the 17th.

The German occupation of the Dodecanese was completed in late November. Strikes by the StG 3 Stukas caused the British to withdraw from Samos and the Italian garrison to surrender on the 22nd. A few days later Do 24T-3 KO+JF crashed while landing near Karlovasi, on the island of Samos, during the evacuation of the wounded, and sank. Three of the four crew members (a reduced crew was often carried on transport missions) were killed. DJ+ZM similarly crashed during a medical evacuation mission to Kapsali, on the island of Kythera, on 23 December, killing three of its full crew of six.

When Italy changed sides in the war, the Germans moved swiftly to take over Italian positions and garrisons, not forgetting those on various small Greek islands. 7. *Staffel* Do 24T-2 CH+EX is seen on a troop transport mission. The aircraft was lost in a fatal take off accident at Naxos on 29 October 1943 (*P Staal*)

The Italian soldiers that surrendered to the Wehrmacht in the Dodecanese were given the choice of continuing to fight on the Axis side or to work in a German labour camp. Most chose the latter,

Seenotstaffel 7 personnel at Athens in January 1944. Oberfeldwebel Wilhelm Lange, fourth from the left, seems to be telling his comrades of his protracted, rather pleasant, ferry trip from Kiel in KO+JC. His Iron Cross-wearing buddy is his namesake, Oberfeldwebel Wilhelm Sommer, another seasoned Do 24 pilot (*H Thürling*)

Assigned to 7. *Staffel*, DJ+ZM saw service both in the Eastern Mediterranean and in the Black Sea. On 22 February 1943 the squadron commander, Hauptmann Hans Tretter, flew this aircraft to Varna, and two days later he continued to Sevastopol to take part in the Kuban airlift. The flying boat is seen back in Athens later in 1943, having just returned from a flight. The new *Staffelkapitän*, Hauptmann Hans Lösch, has joined the motor launch to greet the crew (*H Thürling*)

but the transport of prisoners led to two of the worst maritime disasters of World War 2. On 19 October 1943 the merchantman *Sinfra*, carrying some 2400 prisoners in its hold, as well as 204 Germans, was sunk by USAAF B-25 Mitchells and RAF Beaufighters some 19 miles to the north of Souda Bay. The ship sent an SOS saying 'Save German troops first'. That day, 566 men were rescued, including 163 Germans, but more than 2000 drowned. During the rescue operations a Do 24 from Souda Bay was strafed by Beaufighter Xs of No 603 Sqn. The Dornier was taken in tow by a support boat, but the seaplane sank before reaching its base.

An even worse disaster occurred on 12 February 1944 when the steamer *Oria*, crammed with 4046 Italians and 90 Germans from Rhodes, hit a rock near Patroklos and broke in two. The next morning 28 survivors were rescued by one boat and two Do 24s from nearby Athens. However, more than 4000 people lost their lives.

The crew of Leutnant Walter Kämpf and Feldwebel Wilhelm Lange had a break from the misery of the war when they travelled to Kiel by air and rail to pick up new French-built Do 24T-3 KO+JC in late November 1943. They had some work done on the seaplane at Bramo, near Berlin, and at Dornier in Friedrichshafen. Bad weather delayed their onward flight from Vienna, to the delight of Kämpf who was a Wiener. Another delay allowed them to tour the canals of Venice. Rather dicier was an unplanned stop on the Save River in Bosnia, but they eventually found themselves celebrating Christmas with pro-German villagers, and did not arrive in Athens until the last days of the year, having taken more than four weeks to reach the Mediterranean.

Wearing a fresh squadron code, Do 24T-3 J9+AA was lost on a re-supply flight to Leros on 1 July 1944 when it was strafed and sunk by a British aircraft just after landing in Lakki harbour. The crew escaped with light injuries, being picked up the next day by another Do 24. *Seenotstaffel* 7 was re-designated *Seenotstaffel* 70 on 19 August 1944. It absorbed the remnants of two other *Staffeln*, *Seenotstaffel* 6 from the Adriatic, and *Seenotstaffel* 8, which had been driven out of its 'habitat' of three years, the Black Sea.

SEENOTSTAFFEL 8

On 5 June 1941, a good two weeks before Germany's invasion of the Soviet Union, a flight of He 59s landed at Mamaia, in Rumania, after a 'puddle-hopping' flight. The Siutghiol coastal lake at Mamaia, near the naval base of Constanṭa, was already home to a Rumanian squadron of Savoia-Marchetti SM.55s and SM.62s and Cant Z.501 flying boats, and the Germans based themselves on the other side of the lake.

There was also a land airfield. From Mamaia, the new *Seenotstaffel* 8 was to provide air-sea rescue cover, as well as maritime reconnaissance along the southern flank of the Eastern Front.

Although some small vessels, including *Seenotdienst* boats, were transported overland, Axis warships could not enter the Black Sea through the Turkish Straits, and the Soviet Black Sea fleet thus enjoyed a naval preponderance that encouraged it to bombard Constanţa in the early morning of 26 June – only four days into Operation *Barbarossa*. The heavy destroyer *Moskva* was sunk by a mine or torpedo, however, and *Seenotstaffel* 8's four airworthy He 59s were scrambled to pick up 41 Soviet sailors. The Soviet air forces were also aggressively attacking Rumanian targets early on, and there was no shortage of downed aviators for the Heinkel floatplanes to rescue. Two Arado Ar 196s floatplanes were also assigned to the *Seenotstaffel*, mainly in a maritime reconnaissance capacity.

Two new Do 24T-2s, CM+IV and CM+IZ, joined *Seenotstaffel* 8 at Constanţa on 26 July 1942. The squadron's badge was a skull on a black shield, as seen here on the nose of CM+IV. Put to good use during the Kuban airlift, this aeroplane was transferred to the German Bight in June 1943 and eventually destroyed by a B-17 gunner (*P Staal*)

The first Do 24 for 8. *Staffel*, KK+UV, arrived on 16 August, flying its maiden rescue mission on the 24th. KK+UY also joined the squadron on 20 September. Apparently, these Do 24T-1s developed some problems with their Fafnir engines, for on 3 November KK+UV flew from Mamaia to Constanţa proper to have two of them replaced. The seaplane overturned on landing, however, and all three crewmen on board were killed. The new engines were then fitted to KK+UY instead. To replace the lost aircraft, Do 24T KK+VC transferred from *Seenotstaffel* 7, making a non-stop four-hour flight from Athens to Constanţa on 9 November.

Although the Axis armies had advanced into the Crimea, *Seenotstaffel* 8 had to draw back to Varna, in Bulgaria, on 29 November. The coldest winter of the century had closed in, and ice was causing problems at Mamaia and the unit's forward locations. Indeed, a He 59 had become icebound at Taganrog, and it was guarded by unfortunate soldiers throughout that winter, only to be written off in the spring. Varna got its share of bad weather too, and whilst moored there KK+UY sank in a storm on the night of 30 December. With KK+VC and other aircraft unserviceable, the *Staffel* was reduced to a single airworthy Fw 58 Weihe! Even more worryingly, the young unit had already lost 14 airmen by the turn of the year.

The spring finally came to Constanţa in late March 1942, and KK+VC flew its first mission from the city's port on 2 April, Siutghiol still being frozen. On 6 and 7 April, two new Do 24Ts joined the unit, followed by four more over the next few months. Three new crews also arrived by train from Vienna. On 29 May a Do 24 and a He 59 rescued survivors of the Rumanian merchantman *Sulina*, which had been sunk off Odessa by the Soviet submarine *A-3*.

Earlier in May, newly arrived Do 24 CM+IQ had been based in the Crimea, taking up position in the port of Ak-Metschet (Chornomorske) in order to be closer to the front. A He 59 was based on the salt lake of Saki. On 1 June CM+IQ rescued the crew of a He 111 torpedo-bomber from II./KG 26, which was active around the Crimea. Several crews from KG 26 were rescued by the Do 24s during this period. In one case, the aircraft sprung a leak upon a rough landing in sea state 4-5. Making water, the flying boat still managed to take off and fly to Constanţa, where it was hastily hoisted out of the water by a crane after alighting.

BV 138 flying boats of *Seeaufklärungsgruppe* 125 had, meanwhile, arrived at Mamaia to take over the maritime reconnaissance mission, and on 5 June an extensive search started for a missing 'Flying Clog'. Two survivors were finally found on the 9th.

The great Soviet bastion and port in the Crimea, Sevastopol, finally fell on 4 July. Eighteen German airmen had been rescued by the *Seenotdienst* during the siege of the city, and the reward for *Seenotstaffel* 8 was the seaplane station at Cape Khersones, which became its new main base. Forward locations adopted in the eastern Crimea were Feodosia, Kazantip, on the Sea of Azov, and the Tobechiskoye salt lagoon near Kerch, which the Germans called the Ortasli-See. Early in August both CM+IQ at Feodosia and CM+IZ at Kazantip were damaged by bombs, and both had to be flown to Constanţa, which remained 8. *Seenotstaffel's* maintenance base. A month earlier, on 9 July, CM+IG had been ferried from Ak-Metschet to Mamaia on two engines. Landing late at night, Unteroffizier Ludwig Gosepath swerved to avoid a boat on the lake and ran up onto the beach, causing heavy damage to his Do 24T-2. Gosepath was found guilty of causing the accident and relegated to flying He 59s for some time.

Also in July, German Army Group A took Rostov-on-Don and advanced south into the Caucasus, going for the oil fields of Azerbaijan. In support, the Luftwaffe launched heavy raids against the region's Black Sea ports, including Poti and Batumi, in Georgia, near the Turkish border. The Do 24s flew both maritime reconnaissance and standing rescue patrols, and by mid-September five Dorniers were stationed at the primitive forward base on the Ortasli-See, where one of them was damaged by a Soviet air raid on the 26th. Despite fighter escorts, the Do 24s were often attacked by Soviet fighters. One seaplane that had been shot up was forced to land in Turkish territorial waters. A second Do 24, commanded by Hauptmann Walter Gladigau, came in and rescued the crew. Gladigau's gunners also finished off the stricken Do 24 with cannon fire. Another flying boat was also lost in Turkish waters, its crew reaching the mainland.

Hitler never got the oil fields – the encircling of Stalingrad forced the Germans to pull out of the Caucasus. By January 1943 the 17th Army had dug in behind the Kuban River on the Taman peninsula, across the Kerch Strait from the Crimea, expecting to go on the offensive once again when the weather improved. With the Strait frozen over, an airlift to supply the 17th Army bridgehead started on 4 February. However, the arrival of the spring thaw reduced the capacity of the airfields, and a seaplane airlift was ordered to make up for this. Freshly promoted to major, 8. *Seenotstaffel's Staffelkapitän* Hannibal Gude was put in

Hauptmann Hans Tretter (right), who commanded the Do 24 component of the Kuban airlift, talks to Generalleutnant Martin Fiebig (centre) on board a launch in the Ortasli-See, near Kerch, on 13 March 1943. Fiebig, commander of VIII *Fliegerkorps* in the Stalingrad sector, was executed in Belgrade for war crimes (specifically the bombing of the Yugoslavian capital in 1941) in October 1947. A solitary Do 24 can be seen in the distance on the left. Seaplanes helped to keep the 17th Army supplied during the spring thaw (*P Staal*)

command, and ordered to find a suitable airhead. Leutnant Werner Lange, who served under his leadership, is quoted in *Seaplanes over the Black Sea*;

'On 21 February 1943 I took off from Sevastopol at 0903 hrs in Do 24 CM+IV. Major Gude acted as observer and we landed at 1120 hrs on the Vityazevski Lake. It was risky to land there, as we were not certain of its depth. Finally, we decided to land near the village of Gostagayka as we thought it was the best place, judging from the air. The landing and the taxiing on the lake went smoothly and the people were very friendly. They welcomed us and gave us Kuban wine. On the 28th we returned to Vityazevski and began preparing the site for seaplane operations. On 7 March I took the command of the *Aussenkommando* Ortasli.'

Two *Seetransportstaffeln* were being assembled, one with 20-25 Ju 52/3ms fitted with floats, and the other with 18 Do 24s, seven of them from 8. *Seenotstaffel* and the balance from its sister squadrons around Europe. Doing three or four return flights a day, the seaplanes flew 1910 tonnes of supplies into Gostagayka between 5 and 25 March, when boats could take over from the aircraft. On 9 March a Do 24 flew into a cliff near Feodosia, killing five of its crew. It seems that this aircraft was brand new DJ+ZO of 6. *Staffel*, which had been sent straight from Germany. One Ju 52/3m See was also lost during the airlift, on 23 March – its crew was rescued by Do 24T-2 CM+IV.

The borrowed Do 24s went back to their units, and by early April the strength of *Seenotstaffel* 8 was four Do 24s at the Ortasli-See, two at Sevastopol-Khersones, one at Constanţa and one at Varna – two He 59s remained operational at Constanţa, and there were three Fw 58s at Anapa, on the Taman peninsula. On 15 April, CM+IQ failed to find five crewman from a missing He 111 of 6./KG 55. A promised fighter escort for the mission did not arrive, and although the Do 24T-2 was attacked by Soviet fighters it escaped with only slight damage. The same aircraft scrambled again a few hours later to rescue three German soldiers in a small boat off Mama Russkaya, near Kurortne – a fourth man drowned as he tried to swim to the coast. The flying boat was unable to take off again, so it was taxied into the village's little port.

On 14 June at 0453 hrs VH+SL took off from Ortasli to search for two crewmen from Bf 110 nightfighter 2N+CU that had crashed near Kerch the previous evening while attacking an Il-4 bomber. The seaplane's pilot was Ludwig Gosepath, whose ban on flying the Do 24 had by now been lifted. A survivor was rescued and the flying boat's commander, an enthusiastic Nazi, greeted him with a zealotic 'Heil Hitler' – only to discover that he was a Russian airman! They continued their search and found the Bf 110's radio operator, Unteroffizier Kurt Pfeffers, and subsequently the pilot, Oberleutnant Hans-Jochen Janke. When Pfeffers saw the Russian he attacked him, shouting that the Il-4 had rammed their Bf 110. Gosepath landed VH+SL on the Ortasli-See at 0927 hrs.

Six days later the same Do 24T-3 rescued a Bf 109 pilot from II./JG 3 near Taganrog, and on 1 July it picked up the crew of a Rumanian SM.62 flying boat that had made an emergency landing at sea. One month later, on 1 August, an Ar 196 did the same thing, and again it was VH+SL that rescued the crew – the Arado floatplane was salvaged by a boat.

The Kuban bridgehead was eventually given up in September, and 250,000 troops were evacuated across the Kerch Strait by sea.

On 16 September – the day the Soviets liberated the port of Novorossiysk – a Bf 110 was shot down near there, and CM+IQ, which came to the rescue, was attacked by four Soviet fighters. The pilot of the Do 24, Feldwebel Karl-Heinz Schulze, was killed at the controls, but flight engineer Oberfeldwebel Heinz Baumann and observer Oberleutnant Hans Glinkemann replaced him and managed to land on the Ortasli-See. Another Do 24 went in and rescued the pilot of the Bf 110.

On 9 October the last German army unit successfully crossed the Kerch Strait to the Crimea, and *Seenotstaffel* 8 withdrew from the Ortasli-See, which was now within range of Soviet artillery. Soon, all the Axis forces in the Crimea were cut off by the Red Army's advance into the Ukraine, and they now needed to be supplied by sea and air from Odessa and Rumania. This meant plenty of work for *Seenotstaffel* 8, the strength of which had been reduced to five Do 24s by late October. Two more Dorniers arrived at Varna on the last day of 1943.

As 1944 got under way, the squadron was operating mainly from a lake near Odessa, providing rescue escorts for Ju 52/3m convoys flying in from the Crimea. By mid-January the lake had frozen over, however, and the Do 24s had to relocate to Varna, far away from the convoy route. Even refuelling stops in Odessa's seaport became impossible for several weeks.

Another Do 24, CM+RI, joined *Seenotstaffel* 8 on 13 March, but its arrival was more than nullified by the loss of two aircraft with their entire crews that same day. KO+JP, which had arrived from Norway on 31 December, was shot down by Soviet fighters on a flight from Sevastopol-Khersones, and DJ+ZG probably met the same fate on a sortie from Odessa, notwithstanding an escort of two Bf 110s. Also on the 13th, Do 24 CM+IC rescued five members of a He 111H crew from I./KG 4 – a sixth airman died. Two days later, the medic/tail gunner of lost Do 24 DJ+ZG, *Sanitätsgefreiter* Ottmar Scharrer, was found dead in his dinghy.

On 27 March the Red Army launched an attack in the direction of Odessa, cutting off German troops in the city by 4 April, and two days later three of 8. *Staffel's* handful of Do 24s started flying a minor airlift from Odessa, carrying out 30 tons of radio equipment and 50 Luftwaffe personnel to Galați, in Rumania. This was only a warm-up, however. On 8 April the Soviets also launched an offensive in the Crimea, and two days later the Do 24s were called to Sevastopol to take part in the evacuation of the peninsula – they undertook this task alongside ships and land-based aircraft. Each Do 24 was expected to make three return flights a day to Constanța – a total distance of 1500 miles, or nine hours' flying time. For example, the day's cargo for the *Staffel* on the 12th consisted of 320 soldiers and their equipment.

Well over 200,000 German and Rumanian troops were in the Crimea, and given the magnitude of the task at hand, a substantial fleet of Do 24s was assembled once again – the *Sonderstaffel Mamaia* (Special Squadron) under the command of Hauptmann Heinrich Guthoff. The first two borrowed machines, from *Seenotstaffel* 7, arrived at Constanța-Siutghol on the 15th, followed by six more Do 24s – from *Seenotstaffeln* 6, 9 and 3 – in the next two days.

The flying boats also continued to perform their proper rescue role when required, and on 18 April no less than ten Do 24s headed for the *Alba Iulia*, a Rumanian ship which, carrying some 5000 troops, had been bombed by A-20G Bostons of the Soviet Black Sea Fleet. Many soldiers had jumped overboard, and they were picked up by other vessels and by the German seaplanes. The ship stayed afloat, however, and was towed into Constanţa on the 20th. Do 24 KO+JL was shot down during this operation. A week later, on the 25th, 63 wounded men were rescued from another bombed vessel. On 8 May CM+RB from *Seenotstaffel* 7 was lost to fighters while on its way to a ditched He 111 – four of the Do 24 crew were subsequently found dead and two were classified as missing. On 10 May five Do 24s dropped dinghies and life vests for a large number of survivors of a sunken transport, being unable to land in heavy seas. By the time they returned the next morning all bar seven of the men had died of hypothermia.

The evacuation from the Crimea officially ended the next day. Although thousands of troops perished at sea, some 130,000 escaped to Rumania – 17,000, including 1000 wounded, had been flown out by the Do 24s. In addition to the two aircraft mentioned above, three more Do 24s were lost during the operation – Q8+HA (CM+RH) from *Seenotstaffel* 6 and 1M+DZ from *Seenotstaffel* 8 were destroyed by enemy action at Cape Khersones, and KK+LW collided with an obstacle in the harbour during the night of 9 May. Five men from *Seenotstaffel* 8 and ten other Luftwaffe personnel were killed in this crash. In addition, CM+IC had to be written off after a short circuit fire on board on 28 April.

Sonderstaffel Mamaia was disbanded on 9 June, after which nine of the borrowed Do 24s were returned to their original units, six flying west along the Danube and three going south to *Seenotstaffel* 7 in the Aegean. *Seenotstaffel* 8 was not going to stay in-theatre for much longer either. Perhaps its final rescue action took place on 21 August, when two Do 24s retrieved two BV 138 crews from *Seeaufklärungsgruppe* 125. The latter had lost sight of each other during their patrol, and when one of the seaplanes saw another flying boat it turned out to be a Soviet Catalina. Apparently being used in a rescue role like its German counterpart, the PBY was being escorted by fighters. The latter duly forced both BV 138s down and destroyed them. After hours in the Black Sea, both crews were picked up by a Do 24, which was itself escorted by two Rumanian Bf 109s.

A few days later Germany and Rumania were suddenly at war with each other. As Soviet troops rolled into Rumania, a coup took place in Bucharest and war was declared on Germany. The German lines collapsed, and the Luftwaffe seaplanes and a road column hastily left Constanţa on 25 August. Three Do 24s were ordered to head for Germany, but the balance flew to Salonica, in Greece, before continuing on to Athens-Phaleron on 1 September.

SEENOTSTAFFEL 70

Together with remnants of *Seenotstaffel* 6 from Venice, *Seenotstaffel* 8 was absorbed into *Seenotstaffel* 70, as *Seenotstaffel* 7 had just been re-designated, bringing together a squadron of 19 Do 24s. This could not have happened at a more opportune time, for Greece was being abandoned by the Germans, and the islands, many of them occupied so resolutely just one year earlier, were now being evacuated. On 30 August some 100 Ju 52/3ms started evacuation flights. A unit of seven floatplane Ju 52/3m Sees was also formed to assist the Do 24s in evacuating islands with no airfield.

By the end of October, 37,000 troops had been brought to the mainland by sea and 30,740 by air – some 23,600 troops were left behind on the islands to lead a marginal existence until the end of the war. Most transport flights were done by night, although this did not prevent losses to RAF nightfighters. Nocturnal operations also increased the risk of accidents. The Do 24s typically carried 24 soldiers on these flights, each with 30 kg of equipment, arms and ammunition, which they would badly need during their subsequent retreat through partisan-infested Yugoslavia.

One of *Seenotstaffel* 70's officers was Hauptmann Marijan Gorečan, who was described as a Croatian, although he was likely Slovenian. On 7 September, apparently having had second thoughts about his allegiance, Gorečan and mechanic Feldwebel Karl Mahl hijacked former 6. *Staffel* Do 24N Q8+AB (KD+GF) and flew to Izmir, in Turkey, to declare their wish to defect to the Allies. Three weeks later, on 27 September, Do 24T Q8+AE was damaged in aerial combat near Souda Bay, Crete, and its crew reported the attacker to have been another Do 24 – no doubt Gorečan's! This was clearly a hoax report, however.

The adventures of Do 24T Q8+AE during this period are known in some detail. In September it frequently flew two transport flights a night from Crete, Leros, Samos and Milos, while still on rescue alert and flying rescue missions and additional transport flights by day. After having been damaged by the 'enemy Do 24', Q8+AE was forced down and towed back to Souda Bay. Much the same thing happened just a few days later during the night of 1-2 October, when Q8+AE was forced down off Crete again, although this time the crew of observer Oberfeldwebel Gerhard Huth and pilot Feldwebel Günther Weisshuhn were not sure what had hit them.

Back at Souda, the shot up starboard engine was exchanged with the centre one, allowing them to depart to Athens on two engines during the night of 3-4 October, carrying two army sappers. Near Milos, the unlucky flying boat was attacked by an RAF Beaufighter, which scored multiple hits. Fires were extinguished by the crew and the sappers and burning life vests and dinghies thrown out of the aircraft, while the gunners claimed hits on the nightfighter, which broke off its attack. Making it to Phaleron, Weisshuhn ran his battered machine up on the beach to prevent it from sinking. Only four days later, Q8+AE was back in the air, and it was duly attacked by USAAF P-38 Lightnings while landing at Salonica-Mikra Bay. Again, the flying boat escaped, its less than credible gunners claiming to have shot down no fewer than 13 P-38s between them!

As its squadron code implies, Fokker-built Do 24T-3 Q8+AE previously served with *Seenotstaffel* 6. On 27 April 1944 the aircraft arrived at Varna to be employed in the evacuation of the Crimea. In June it flew to Athens to join *Seenotstaffel* 70, and its adventures in the Aegean are detailed in the text. The flying boat is seen at Athens-Phaleron with a Ju 52/3m See – Do 24s and floatplane Ju 52s often worked shoulder to shoulder in the seaborne airlifts in the Black Sea and Aegean in the final years of the war (*P Staal*)

On 10 October the German retreat from Athens began, the main body of *Seenotstaffel* 8 departing from Phaleron Bay for Salonica in the early hours of the 12th. Q8+AE had now run out of luck, however, and it crashed during a night landing at Salonica – its crew escaped unhurt.

Numerous other Do 24s were also lost during this episode. 1M+AC (KK+UV) crashed at night, landing in Souda Bay on 20 September, only the tail gunner surviving. Six days later another former *Seenotstaffel* 8 aircraft, 1M+RR, was probably shot down en route to Souda Bay – its crew is still missing. During the night of 1-2 October, J9+CA, carrying 22 troops from Souda Bay, was shot down by a British nightfighter near Milos. An able pilot, Oberfeldwebel Wilhelm Lange managed to put his damaged aircraft down on the water. The radio operator and the tail gunner, who had been badly wounded or killed, went down with the flying boat. The remaining four members of the crew and all the soldiers got out, but the latter, having kapok life vests of limited endurance, probably all drowned while the airmen in their dinghies made it to the nearby islands, where the observer, Oberfeldwebel Bernhard Fuhrmann, was thrown against the rocks and killed. On 6 October 1M+RK was shot down by a Mosquito XIII of No 256 Sqn to the south of Zakynthos, killing all six crew. Finally, on the 10th, J9+FA crashed on takeoff from Milos, perhaps overloaded with fuel as Phaleron was running out of petrol. Note that Q8+A. and 1M+. codes were still being worn by the former 6. and 8. *Staffel* machines.

Meanwhile, rescue missions were still being flown. On 6 October Gerhard Huth's crew in Do 24 J9+DA searched for a He 111 crew that had been reported floating in the Aegean off Volos – they had already paddled ashore by the time the seaplane reached the area. J9+DA duly landed at Salonica. That night the minelayer *Zeus* made its way into Salonica with 1125 evacuees, three of its escorts having been sunk by the British destroyers HMS *Termagant* and HMS *Tuscan*. The next morning J9+EA rescued 27 survivors from the torpedo boat *TA-37* (formerly an Italian naval vessel), who were flown to Salonica – 103 of the ship's 142-man crew perished.

On 17 October – the date the Royal Navy sailed into Phaleron Bay – two Do 24s carrying wounded from the city of Volos were intercepted by RAF fighters. Although CM+IQ was shot down with no survivors, J9+EA made it to Salonica, where dorsal gunner Unteroffizier Fritz Becker died of his wounds.

Only six of *Seenotstaffel* 70's 19 Do 24s were left by 23 October, plus two of the seven Ju 52/3m See floatplanes. That night the Do 24s departed Salonica for Germany, the seaplanes initially flying to Vienna. Two of the flying boats had to land prematurely, however, at Vukovar and on Lake Balaton, respectively. On the 26th, four or five of the Do 24s arrived at the Chiemsee, in Bavaria, only to be destroyed there by British fighter-bombers. After an eventful journey through Yugoslavia, the squadron's road column arrived in nearby Bad Aibling, where the *Staffel* was disbanded.

CHAPTER SIX

BALTIC THEATRE AND SPECIAL OPERATIONS

A fine photograph of Do 24T-2 CM+IA flying over Lake Constance, where 9. *Staffel* held a training camp during the severe winters of 1941 and 1942 (*T Postma*)

The invasion in the Soviet Union also meant the commencing of hostilities in the Baltic Sea and the Gulf of Finland, and *Seenotstaffel* 9 was raised to provide air-sea rescue cover here. The rapid Axis advance to the gates of Leningrad meant that fighting over the Baltic quickly died down, and the squadron assumed a training role. By 1944 the Germans were getting rolled back, however, and *Seenotstaffel* 2 moved into the area from the North Sea coast, merging with *Seenotstaffel* 9 into the new *Seenotstaffel* 81. Heavily involved in the evacuation of German civilians fleeing from the Red Army, this unit flew its final mission weeks *after* the end of the war.

In 1944 two Do 24s also entered service with the secretive *Kampfgeschwader* 200 for special operations behind enemy lines and, as the war drew to its close, four of the flying boats came close to being used in an improbable suicide operation called *Aktion 24*.

SEENOTSTAFFEL 9

The Baltic did not have an air-sea rescue squadron of its own from the spring of 1940, when the He 59s of *Seenotflugkommando* 2 were sent west. On 1 June 1941, however, *Seenotstaffel* 9 was raised to safeguard the *Barbarossa* operations along the Baltic coastlines. Training took place at Warnemünde, near Rostock, and soon the new *Staffel* moved up to the Stintsee (Kis Lake) at Riga, with detachments at Pernau (Pärnu) and Haapsal (Haapsalu) in Estonia. Its aircraft were a handful of He 59s, two Do 18s and two Do 24s. As the command post's radio transmitter had broken down, the Philips radio in one of the Do 24s was used for some time, chaining this aircraft to a telephone line at Riga.

The remaining Do 24 was sent to equip a detachment in Helsinki. The rocky bottom of the Finnish capital's harbour was not kind to the *Seenotdienst* aircraft, however, even though the Suomenlimna base was in regular use by Finnish seaplanes. When the Do 24's hull was ripped open, a local shipyard fixed it by welding a thick steel plate on. Soon the aircraft was leaking again, and it had to retire to Germany for repairs. A Do 18 was based in Helsinki as a replacement, but it crashed, and the He 59 that was sent in next tore open its floats on 17 September. A second He 59 was seriously damaged at Pernau that same day, and another had been shot down by Soviet ground fire 24 hours earlier, causing an acute aircraft shortage for the *Staffelkapitän*, Hauptmann Karl Born.

Working-up of the new *Seenostaffel* 9 took place at Warnemünde, near Rostock, and the golden griffon from that city's coat of arms combined with the golden rune of life to create the squadron badge. The *Staffelkapitän*, Hauptmann Karl Born, had his Do 24s named after German merchant ships (*Seeflieger.de*)

In early December the *Staffel* flew search and rescue missions to pick up survivors of the Soviet liner *Joseph Stalin*, which had run into a minefield during the evacuation of the Soviet-occupied Hanko (Hangö) peninsula. The ship stranded on the Estonian shore, and of the 5500 Red Army troops on board, about a third were rescued by the Soviets, a third killed and a third captured by the Germans.

The freezing of the Gulf of Finland ended operations here, causing *Seenotstaffel* 9 to withdraw to Kiel. The severe frost even prompted a winter training camp at Lake Constance, the personnel enjoying the lodging of the luxury Kurgarten Hotel in Friedrichshafen and the flying boats the maintenance support of the Dornier-Werke GmbH. This was repeated

Do 24s of 9. *Staffel* and an Ar 196 in front of their hangar at Kiel-Holtenau, photographed from the seaplane crane. Frontline units did not always enjoy such excellent facilities (*Seeflieger.de*)

the following winter. Meanwhile, the Baltic was an Axis lake, with minefields locking up the Soviet Baltic Fleet in Leningrad and Kronstadt. Consequently, 9. *Staffel's* operational role was a limited one from 1942. It was based mainly at Kiel, acting as the *Lehr- und Erganzungsstaffel*, tasked with training crews and evaluating new equipment and procedures. New Do 24s from the factories in Holland and France were also broken in by the unit, and sometimes ferried to the frontline squadrons around Europe by 9. *Staffel* crews. A few Do 18s were also in service for lead-in training.

The unit continued to operate in these roles until January 1945 when it was disbanded. An operational squadron, *Seenotstaffel* 81, sprouted from *Seenotstaffel* 9 in August 1944.

SEENOTSTAFFEL 2

The Baltic had become a war zone again in 1944, following the relief of Leningrad in January. On the other hand, there was little German activity left to cover from the Dutch North Sea coast, so 2. *Staffel* left Amsterdam-Schellingwoude for the Baltic in May. Based in the western Baltic area, the unit was formally headquartered at Grossenbrode. Its merits here include the rescue of a B-24 Liberator crewman on 4 August 1944.

At least two 2. *Staffel* aircraft were also flying in the Gulf of Finland from May 1944, Do 24T-3 DT+HA being based in the fishing village of Kunda on the Estonian coast, near the Narva Front. It had a truly Greater German crew – observer Obergefreiter Emil Wagner was from Poland, radio operator Oberfeldwebel Josef König was from the Alsace and flight engineer Gefreiter Henri Dannemark was from German-annexed Eupen-Malmedy, in Belgium. On 25 May these men rescued a Ju 87 pilot, and on 5 June they took to the air to search for the crew of another Stuka, receiving an escort of Fw 190s. They were shot down west of the island of Vigrund, however, by Lavochkin La-5s of the Baltic Fleet. The only survivor, Dannemark, was rescued by another Do 24 that evening after some ten hours in the water. The latter machine may have been KO+IJ or KO+JJ, the presence of which was reported to the Finns.

Five Do 24s show up in the area in Finnish records for July and August 1944, wearing *Seenotstaffel* 2 codes S5+BK, CK, EK, GK and LK. S5+EK was based at Reval (Tallin) from mid-July, performing numerous missions and rescuing the crew of a Do 217 at 2110 hrs on 1 August. Meanwhile, a Soviet spearhead reached the Gulf of Riga, threatening to cut off German Army Group North in Estonia. On 16 August S5+EK flew to Riga and mounted a rescue mission for the crews of several Ju 52/3m and Me 323 transport aircraft – nine men were rescued after a night landing at sea. Me 323 C8+GR of *Transportfliegerführer* 5's II. *Gruppe* crashed on a flight from Riga the following day.

During the night of 17-18 August, while laying a fresh minefield off Narva, three German torpedo boats went adrift and were all blown up by their own mines. Do 24T S5+LK took off from Reval at 0420 hrs and found 'some 250' men squeezed together on rafts and floating in the water. Most of the sailors drowned, but by 1100 hrs the next day pilot Feldwebel Heinz-Ottokar Hildebrandt and his crew had rescued 90 survivors, 50 of which were carried in a single flight. The crew spent the next day cleaning their fuel oil-stained flying boat. Another seven men were apparently rescued by S5+EK, which had returned from Riga to join the operation.

S5+EK, still based at Reval, flew an unsuccessful mission in search of a Soviet Boston bomber crew on 14 September. The Do 24s were now increasingly flown in the transport role, however, joining a sealift in which 85,000 Germans were taken out of Estonia. The last convoy, carrying 9000 soldiers, left Reval on the 23rd. S5+EK had flown 50 passengers from Reval to Riga on the 19th, and five days later it took 53 evacuees from Riga to Libau (Liepaja). The Soviets reached the coast to the south of Libau on 10 October, trapping German Army Group North in the Courland peninsula.

In August *Seenotstaffel* 2 had been disbanded to merge into the new *Seenotstaffel* 81 at Bug, on Rügen, while *Seenotstaffel* 60 at Pillau (Baltiysk) was a continuation, officially, of 1. *Staffel*, which had withdrawn from Lake Biscarosse. The flying element of *Seenotstaffel* 60 was a phantom unit, however, as all the rescue Do 24s still flying in the Baltic were treated as the property of *Seenotstaffel* 81.

SEENOTSTAFFEL 81

Created from 9. *Staffel* in August 1944, and absorbing the remains of 2. *Staffel*, *Seenotstaffel* 81 gathered a fleet of some 14 Do 24s at its main base at Bug, on the island of Rügen. Like *Seenotstaffel* 80 on the North Sea coast, the squadron was given a search and escort component of Me 410 fighters – these were flown by *Such- und Begleitstaffel* 81 at Parow, near Bug. Due to fuel shortages, the Messerschmitts could only be employed sporadically, however.

A second desertion involving a Do 24 occurred on 31 October when flight engineer Heinz Roesch, while based at the *Aussenstelle* Nest near Köslin (Koszalin), hijacked Do 24T-2 CM+RY with his Estonian girlfriend, Rita Kuusalu. Assisted only by her, Roesch, who did not have a pilot's licence, managed to land off Sölvesborg, in Sweden, where the couple and the flying boat were interned. In the same area on 3 April 1945, a Swedish Reggiane Re.2000 fighter was shot down by a flying boat identified as a Do 24 by one of the Swedish pilots involved in this incident.

The Red Army's major offensive of January 1945 destroyed the last German hopes of stopping the Soviets, setting in motion a stream of refugees. During the last 125 days of the war more than two million fleeing Germans were taken out of besieged Baltic ports by sea, and the boats and aircraft of *Seenotgruppe* 81 were heavily involved in rescue and transport operations.

During the evening of 30 January, the notorious sinking of the cruise ship *Wilhelm Gustloff* by a Soviet submarine led to the death of 10,000 people. The Do 24s were unable to contribute to the rescue effort, as related by the *Staffelkapitän*, Hauptmann Siegfried Körner, in the booklet *Seenotgruppe 81/Ostsee 1944/45*;

'According to my logbook I took off from Bug/Rügen at 0520 hrs, joined by two other Do 24s. The day broke slowly as we reached the search area. We conducted our search, flying at an altitude of about 20-25 metres. We could not risk landing as the sea was littered with wreckage. We returned to base at 0920 hrs, having accomplished nothing.'

During the final months of the war, more than two million desperate German civilians massed in Baltic ports besieged by the Soviets, and an estimated 5000 wounded soldiers and children were flown out by *Seenotstaffel* 81 Do 24s. This photograph was taken on the Vistula Split (*T Postma*)

The main operation conducted by *Seenotstaffel* 81 was a medical evacuation from Pillau-Neutief, an airfield and seaplane station with two concrete runways on the tip of the Vistula Spit, across from the East Prussian port of Pillau. The base had been of little importance during the war, but now Pillau and Neutief became major assembly points for the refugees, with local air defence provided by JG 51 'Mölders'. Pillau held out until 25 April, and some 450,000 people were shipped to the West, plus 5000 wounded and sick transported to Rügen on board the Do 24s.

The coastal region of Kolberg (Kołobrzeg) was home to several *KLV-Lager*, in which Berlin children were lodged to shield them from Allied bombing. Early in March children and nurses fleeing from the advancing Soviets flooded the region's two seaplane stations at Nest and Kamp. By now acting on his own discretion, *Seenotgruppe* 81 commander Karl Born ordered his Do 24s into action. When landing at Nest, the crews could see the enemy tanks. About 70 children per flight were taken on board, the overloaded aircraft barely clearing the coastal dunes on the Jamunder See (Jamno Lake) on takeoff. One flying boat arrived at Bug carrying 17 adults and 99 children. The situation at Kamp was very similar. Crammed with 72 evacuees, one of the tail-heavy Do 24s stalled on takeoff here and crashed into the Kamper See on 5 March. Oberfeldwebel Erich Kittner's Do 24 crew taxied to the disaster site and managed to rescue one woman. Kittner then returned to the lakeshore to continue the evacuation. It is estimated that perhaps as many as 2000 children were taken out of the two locations.

On 3 May at Grossenbrode, east of Kiel, two Do 24s were claimed destroyed in a strafing attack by French ace Pierre Clostermann, flying a Tempest V of No 3 Sqn. The next day, as the Red Army approached Rügen,

A Do 24 abandoned on the Schlei at Schleswig after the remarkable formation flight from Denmark, which took place six weeks after the end of the war. The gun turrets had been removed from this aeroplane at some point (*P Dupont*)

Karl Born ordered his aircraft and boats to cross the Baltic to Guldborg, in German-occupied Denmark. During the morning of 5 May 15 Do 24s and one Ar 196 floatplane landed in the Guldborgsund. It meant the end of the war for their crews as the surrender of German forces in Western Europe, including Denmark, took effect at 0800 hrs that very morning.

The Germans had not yet surrendered elsewhere, however, and as mentioned previously, at least one Do 24 from *Seenotstaffel* 50 at Oslo had flown to Windau (Ventspils) in the Courland Pocket. On the orders of Admiral Dönitz, soldiers who had large families were to be flown out to Kiel. Commanded by Unteroffizier Paul Blum, Do 24T-3 5W+BU (CM+IH) loaded 37 fathers from a flak unit and took off during the night of 8-9 May. Instead of heading to Kiel, they landed at Trelleborg, in Sweden, however, apparently due to a navigational error. This mistake was to have grave consequences for the four crew and the evacuees, since all German soldiers who escaped to Sweden from the Baltic states were extradited to the Soviet Union after the end of the war.

Even *Seenotstaffel* 81, now under Allied control at Guldborg, had not yet flown its last mission. With British approval, all 15 Do 24s flew to Schleswig, in Germany, on 18 June 1945, repatriating 450 wounded German soldiers from Danish hospitals. Swastikas had been removed and Red Cross markings applied on the Do 24s by order of the British, who provided an escort of 16 Typhoons. It was the very last mission undertaken by the Luftwaffe, and a fitting swansong for the *Seenotdienst* (*Luft*).

Seenotdienst aircraft and boats rescued 11,561 survivors from the sea during World War 2, according to German records – this figure excludes mere evacuations from ships, and includes 3815 Allied personnel rescued (and/or captured). Of that total, 1665 were rescued off Western European shores, 3200 from Norwegian waters, 4113 from the Mediterranean, 545 from the Black Sea and 2038 from the German Bight and off Baltic shores.

KAMPFGESCHWADER 200

During 1944 two Do 24s served with a seaplane squadron of the Luftwaffe special operations unit, *Kampfgeschwader* 200. In March 1944 3./KG 200

The Luftwaffe's famous secretive unit KG 200 used seaplanes for the insertion of agents behind Soviet lines in 1944. Two Do 24s were assigned to its seaplane squadron, including A3+EE, which was flown from Bug on Rügen to Schleswig on 1 May 1945. It was photographed there by a British soldier after the war had ended (*D Lilly*)

was formed at Bug, and equipped with two French four-engined Lioré et Olivier LeO H-246 flying boats, an He 115, an Ar 196 and the two Do 24s. Led by an officer named Theodor Queens, parts of the squadron were sent to Kupoio-Rissala airfield and seaplane station in eastern Finland in June 1944. Their mission was the insertion of spies or saboteurs behind Soviet lines, in close cooperation with Finnish forces. A remote base on the lake of Tiiksjärvi (Tikshozero), in northern Karelia, was used as a staging point, and thus the action was perhaps related to the Murmansk railway line. One of the LeO H-246s crashed while in Finland, and some KG 200 personnel travelled by ship when the unit returned to Germany in September. As the Red Army approached Rügen, 3./KG 200's surviving aircraft were flown from Bug to Schleswig on 1 May 1945, and one of its Do 24s, coded A3+EE, was among the flying boats lying abandoned there after the capitulation.

Following its unsuccessful use of unmanned *Mistel* Ju 88s as flying bombs, KG 200 was also associated with an improbable suicide operation, *Aktion 24*. Crammed with explosives, four Do 24s were to land on the Vistula River at Torún, Warsaw, Deblin and Kraków, where they were to be blown up against or under major bridges in order to slow down the Soviet advance. The four *Seenotdienst* pilots selected for this job apparently declined the offer to earn a posthumous Knight's Cross, however. They were then ordered to land on the river and to exit into hostile territory, leaving the blowing-up bit to inexperienced, but more fanatical co-pilots.

The first Do 24s arrived at the Rechlin test base, which possessed a seaplane ramp on the Müritz Lake, in mid-March 1945, and three more flew in on 1 April. Non-essential equipment and gun turrets were removed, and boxes filled with dynamite and magnesium were installed and linked to a fuse that ran into the cockpit. By 25 April, three of the suicide flying boats were hiding in a bay of the lake near Röbel, and the fourth, Do 24T-1 KK+VC, was taxiing there to join the others when it was attacked by P-51 Mustangs of the USAAF's 354th Fighter Squadron. The dynamite did not explode, but the Do 24 was destroyed and the pilot killed. He was Feldwebel Heinz-Ottokar Hildebrandt, who had saved the lives of 90 seamen with his *Seenotstaffel* 2 crew off Narva in August 1944. *Aktion 24* was not carried out, and Hildebrandt's three colleagues flew to Bug in one of the surviving Do 24s.

CHAPTER SEVEN

OTHER OPERATORS

lthough the Dutch navy in the East Indies and the *Seenotdienst* of the Luftwaffe were the principal operators of the Do 24, the flying boat saw service with several other air arms. The first of these was the Royal Australian Air Force (RAAF), which flew a handful of former Dutch aircraft after the occupation of the NEI. It is unknown what happened to the Do 24N of Hauptmann Gorečan, who deserted to Turkey in 1944. The aircraft used by Heinz Roesch, however, was impressed into the Swedish air force, and the other Do 24 that landed in Sweden even ended up in Soviet service. Two German machines left behind in Norway saw some local use after the end of the war, and three Do 24s were flown to the UK for evaluation. More substantial was the use of the Do 24 by the French navy, as 40 aircraft were built for the *Aéronavale* by the *Société Nationale de Constructions Aéronautiques du Nord* (SNCAN) after the war. The longevity prize, however, goes to the Spanish air force, which used the type from 1944 into the late 1960s.

The Australian Do 24s were unarmed, but retained their Alkan turrets. The dorsal turret was unbolted for the loading and unloading of troops, mail and cargo. A49-4 was retired in early 1944 (*T Postma*)

AUSTRALIA

Only six of the Dutch Do 24s survived their escape to Australia, as detailed in Chapter 3. All were in a sorry condition by the time they reached RAAF Rathmines seaplane station on Lake Macquarie, in New South Wales. Plans to restart Dutch flying training in Australia encountered other difficulties, too, and as a Dutch military flying school was set up in Texas, the six aircraft were offered for sale to the RAAF, which was very short of equipment, in April 1942. The Dutch stated that the purchase price had been the equivalent of £57,200 for those machines built in Germany and £81,900 for those manufactured in Holland, although in reality all six seaplanes had come from the Swiss Dornier plant. Their condition was so poor that their residual value was agreed to be only £9380 per aircraft, or £46,900 for five – the Dutch requested to retain X-24 after all for flights on behalf of their NEFIS intelligence service. The others, X-5 and X-7 through to X-10, became A49-1 through to -5.

The six aircraft received an overhaul with No 1 Flying Boat Repair Depot (FBRD) at Lake Boga, Victoria, and X-24 was returned to the Dutch navy on 8 June. Four days earlier, X-8, now A49-3, had become the first Do 24 to fly in RAAF service when it took off for a test flight. The pilot was Sqn Ldr Bryan Monkton, whose comment on the arrival of the Dutch crews at Rathmines was quoted in Chapter 3.

The Australian intention was to use the Do 24s in the transport and advanced training roles, thus freeing up Catalinas for operational duties. They were initially assigned to No 9 Sqn, the RAAF's fleet cooperation unit (which flew Seagull V and Walrus amphibians), the Rathmines Station Headquarters and No 3 Operational Training Unit. The Do 24s saw little or no use with any of these outfits, however, as serviceability was appalling. From September 1942 the five flying boats were rotated through a more thorough overhaul that saw them converted into Do 24T transport aircraft. Carried out both by No 1 FBRD at Lake Boga and No 2 FBRD at Rathmines, this job took until October 1943 to complete. The flying boats' hulls were completely re-plated, and the electrical wiring that was sensitive to salt water corrosion was stripped and replaced. The gun turrets were retained, although armament was no longer carried.

Not all serviceability problems could be solved, however. The Dutch had already suffered from the non-availability of spare parts, even for the American-built R-1820-F52 Cyclone engines that were long out of production. Moreover, the RAAF had little information on how to operate or maintain German-built flying boats. Despite ongoing technical issues, the Dorniers were issued to No 41 Sqn. Since the outbreak of war, the RAAF had raised several transport units, and in August 1942 No 41 Sqn had spawned from No 33 Sqn, operating two former Qantas Short Empire flying boats from Townsville, on the Queensland coast. From here, the squadron maintained important air links between Australia and Port Moresby and Milne Bay in eastern New Guinea, transporting troops, army mail and urgent cargoes.

The war was going badly for the Allies in the southwest Pacific, as the Japanese had landed at Buna and Gona on the north coast of eastern New Guinea, and were advancing towards Moresby through rugged jungle terrain. However, a direct Japanese attack against Milne Bay failed in August 1942.

A49-3 was the first Do 24 to come out of overhaul, being test flown by Monkton and his crew at Lake Boga on 4 June 1943. They departed for Townsville

The former X-10, A49-5/DQ-H of No 41 Sqn in flight over the Australian outback. The RAAF Do 24s were used to supply troops fighting in eastern New Guinea, but maintenance visits to Lake Boga, Victoria, were all too common. This machine caught fire while refuelling at Darwin on 11 May 1944 (*Aviation Heritage Museum of Western Australia*)

three days later, but engine trouble soon bobbed up again. The flying boat finally reached No 41 Sqn on the 10th, and flew its first transport mission to Port Moresby three days later – by then it was wearing the No 41 Sqn code DQ-F. A49-5 was the next to arrive, but this aircraft's maiden mission to Port Moresby on 27 June was aborted due to engine problems. Two days later an engine cowling came loose, and shortly thereafter the aircraft was grounded due to electrical defects. It was sent back to Lake Boga, but the repair job was unsuccessful as electrical faults resurfaced even before the flying boat had returned to Townsville. It resumed operational flights to Port Moresby on 27 September – only to be damaged by a refuelling barge at Cairns three days later.

Meanwhile, A49-4 had joined No 41 Sqn on 4 August, although this aircraft had also experienced technical problems during its ferry flight. Finally, A49-1 and A49-2 reached Townsville in October – the latter aircraft had already been in use as a crew trainer at Rathmines for some time. A49-1 had an engine replaced at Brisbane, just hours after coming out of overhaul. This flying boat also suffered from excessive fuel consumption, and it was taken out of service several times in vain attempts to rectify the problem. The Dutch special missions aircraft X-24 suffered from the same condition, and it saw no more service after it was given to the RAAF in October 1943, becoming A49-6.

Philip Mathieson flew the Do 24 with No 41 Sqn, and he made some interesting observations about the seaplane in a 1960s interview in *Man & Aerial Machine* magazine, including some criticism of the type's much-praised behaviour in the water;

'The Dornier was quite a change from the Empire boats, where you were sitting fairly high out of the water. With the Dornier, you could reach out through your window and touch the water. The Dornier had a very sharp bow, with a turret up forward so that you were blind straight ahead. It had a fairly flat bottom, just a shallow V, and it was quite good in reasonable weather conditions, in a chop, but it wasn't particularly good if you had to operate in a swell. It could get down into very rough conditions because you could stall it in, but whether you would get out is another thing.

'On takeoff in rough conditions you were completely blind from the water because you would cut straight through the waves, and the green water, fishes and everything else would come back over the top until she climbed up on the step and got running on top of the sea.

'They were very, very strong aircraft, but what I didn't like about them was that the hull was somewhat reminiscent of a submarine. It was quite a low, tubular sort of fuselage, and you went down into it through a round hatch. And what would have happened had anyone had an accident on landing or takeoff, I hate to think. I don't believe anyone would have gotten out of it – they were all well and truly battened down inside.'

No 41 Sqn's S 23 Empires were returned to Qantas in July 1943, and thus the unit solely operated Do 24s when the Allies went on the offensive on the north coast of New Guinea that summer. Goodenough Island, Finschhafen and Salamaua now figured on the squadron's roster, as did Nouméa, in French Caledonia, which hosted an important Allied base. Although serviceability improved somewhat as experience with the German aircraft grew, it never reached an acceptable level.

Derelict Dorniers at Lake Boga. The second aircraft is the Dutch special operations machine X-24, which was given to the RAAF on 8 October 1943 (*P Staal*)

Twelve Martin PBM-3R Mariner transport flying boats were delivered to the RAAF from late 1943 and allocated to No 41 Sqn and its new sister unit, No 40. These voluminous and more reliable machines quickly replaced the Do 24s in the transport role, and by early 1944 the latter were dedicated to search and rescue duties. A29-2 and A29-4 could no longer be kept operational, however, and were retired to Lake Boga.

On the second day of 1944, A49-3 flew from Townsville to Moresby, Milne Bay, Goodenough Island and finally to Kiriwina, in the Trobriand Islands, to assess the feasibility of establishing a rescue flight there. The Allies had landed on Kiriwina on 30 June 1943 and quickly constructed an airfield that was used by RAAF combat squadrons, as well as a seaplane jetty. A49-5 was sent west to Darwin on 9 January, staging through Karumba and Groote Eylandt, and arriving on the 11th. From Darwin it served as the rescue aircraft for HQ North-Western Area, detached to No 52 Operations Base Unit. It apparently rescued an A-20 Boston crew as No 41 Sqn received a message of thanks of this import on 29 March.

Meanwhile, A49-3 had taken up the rescue duty at Kiriwina, having returned to the island on 9 February. On the 5th and 6th it conducted a search for a missing aircraft from Milne Bay. On Kiriwina it was detached to No 8 Communications Unit. On 16 March A49-1 arrived at Kiriwina to relieve its sister aircraft, and the following day, the seaplane rescued the crew of A-20C Boston A28-24 of Kiriwina-based No 22 Sqn. A49-1 flew its last operational mission from Kiriwina on 22 May 1944, ending the two-year saga of the combat-weary Dornier flying boats in RAAF service. Despite all their malfunctions, the aircraft had operated without any serious accidents until 11 May, when A49-5 caught fire and sank in Darwin Harbour while refuelling. Serious burns were sustained by the Do 24's radio operator, Flt Sgt Wall, and two electrical mechanics, so an electrical fault was the likely cause.

The remaining Do 24s were put in storage at Lake Boga, and struck off charge and scrapped before the end of the year. Only A49-6 escaped the wrecker, perhaps because it was possibly still Dutch-owned, the seaplane ending its days as a playground attraction in Blackalls Park on Lake Macquarie. The nose section of one of the aircraft survived to be turned into a boat, and it is now an exhibit in the Lake Boga Flying Boat Museum in Victoria.

SWEDEN AND THE SOVIET UNION

Two German Do 24s ended up in neutral Sweden in the final phase of the war in Europe, as described in Chapter 6, and both aircraft saw extended service. On 31 October 1944 a flight engineer serving with *Seenotstaffel* 81, Heinz Roesch, and his Estonian girlfriend, Rita Kuusalu, hijacked CM+RY, a relatively new Fokker-assembled Do 24T-3 stationed at Nest, on the coast of Pomerania. Without the benefit of a pilot's licence, Roesch successfully

landed near Sölvesborg, in Blekinge
province. The flying boat was
interned, and Nazi Germany was
paid 250,000 kronor for it to
appease both warring sides.

The love story between Roesch
and Rita Kuusalu did not have a
happy ending, but at least Heinz got
himself a job out of his desertion.
Having considerable experience as a
Do 24 flight engineer, he was hired as an advisor when CM+RY entered
service with the Swedish air force in the search and rescue role. It was issued
to the F2 wing at Hägernäs seaplane base, near Stockholm, in May 1945
following an overhaul at Västerås. Given the type designation Tp 24, the
Do 24 flew 135 hours in 1945-46 and 119 in 1947. Early in 1948 three
PBY-5A Canso amphibians were purchased from Canada to take over the
search and rescue role, relegating the Do 24 to second fiddle. Its maintenance
costs also began to rise steeply, and the Do 24 was scrapped in 1951.

Interned in Sweden after Heinz Roesch's
desertion, one Do 24T-3 served with the
F2 wing at Stockholm-Hägernäs for
several years. Initially painted in a black-
green 'submarine' colour scheme, it was
later stripped to bare metal (*T Postma*)

Another Luftwaffe Do 24 landed in Sweden on 9 May 1945. Previously
based in Norway, 5W+BU was on an evacuation flight from Windau
(Ventspils, in Latvia) when Unteroffizier Paul Blum's crew of four
apparently ended up at Trelleborg due to a navigational error, carrying 37
German soldiers who were fathers of large families. All on board were
interned in Sweden. In June 1945, however, the Soviet government
demanded the extradition of all Axis soldiers who had fled to Sweden from
the Baltic states, which were Soviet lands according to Moscow. Stockholm
complied, and Blum and his crew and passengers were among some 3000
Germans shipped to the Soviet Union. The Do 24 was also handed over
to the USSR on 14 August 1945 and flown off by a Soviet crew. Despite
the abundance of good aircraft available to the Russians, the single Do 24
flew with Polar Aviation in Siberia for several years.

NORWAY AND GREAT BRITAIN

Mine clearing operations in Norwegian waters after the end of the war
required rescue cover, and two Do 24T-3s of *Seenotstaffel* 51, surrendered
at Tromsø on 8 May 1945, were put to work by the British. The two
aircraft, CM+RE and CM+RR, were allegedly painted white, flying with
their German crews without an Allied supervisor on board. They moved
to Oslo-Fornebu in the autumn of 1945, and although still manned by
German crews, a Norwegian officer now came on board for each flight.
The aircraft formally belonged to No 333 (Norwegian) Sqn, which
operated Catalinas. As environmental awareness or a sense of aviation
history had not arrived yet, they were both scuttled at Horten in February
1946. Two Do 24s surrendered at Bodø are also said to have been used
locally by the British, but this might refer to the same aircraft.

Three of the Do 24T-3s abandoned on the Schlei at Schlesswig were
earmarked for British evaluation. Two of these aircraft, P7+MN and
VH+JM of *Seenotstaffel* 81, had taken part in its final flight from Denmark
on 18 June 1945. The third Do 24 was one of the two special missions

Taken in 1947, this photograph shows Soviet-seized Do 24 5W+BU on the Yenisei River at Igarka, some 1500 miles northeast of Moscow. It is wearing Soviet stars that have been applied directly over its Luftwaffe markings (*P Dupont*)

aircraft assigned to KG 200. They received the British serials AM114/VN865, AM116/VN870 and AM115/VM483, respectively. Canadian pilot Sqn Ldr Ian 'Curly' Somerville of the Royal Aircraft Establishment's Foreign Aircraft Flight test-flew the latter machine at Schleswig on 16 July 1945. Ferried to Felixstowe, it sank in a gale on 2 October 1945. The remaining two Do 24s were flown to the Marine Experimental Establishment at Felixstowe on 6 December 1945, where VN865 was allocated to type trials and VN870 used for tests with its air-sea rescue equipment. By June 1946 they were no longer airworthy, and both were scrapped at J Dale & Co in late 1947.

FRANCE

The German occupiers made arrangements for the CAMS seaplane factory at Sartrouville, near Paris, to join the Do 24T production programme for the *Seenotdienst* in July 1941, although the first aircraft, CM+IJ, was not launched into the Seine until October 1942 – and it was still assembled from Dutch-manufactured parts. Subsequently, 47 machines were fabricated in France until Paris was liberated in August 1944, by which point Do 24 production was about to be terminated anyway. The French government decided, however, to continue production of several German aircraft built in French factories, including the Do 24T. The usefulness of these aeroplanes was of secondary importance – the main motivation was to get the industry going again post-war.

Thus, the CAMS factory, which belonged to SNCAN (later renamed Nord-Aviation) delivered 39 or 40 Do 24s to the French naval air service, the *Aéronavale*. The first two deliveries took place in late December 1944, followed by seven more in the first quarter of 1945. The very last Do 24 was delivered on 15 July 1947. Gun turrets were installed, but they were sometimes removed, and the dorsal gunner's position was used

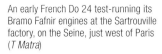

An early French Do 24 test-running its Bramo Fafnir engines at the Sartrouville factory, on the Seine, just west of Paris (*T Matra*)

– in some of the aircraft at least – as a radar operator's station for the primitive British ASV (Air to Surface Vessel) radar sets that had been installed on board.

The first *Aéronavale* squadron to be equipped with the Do 24 was *Flottille* 9FTr, a transport unit raised on 1 November 1944 at St-Mandrier, near Toulon. Its task was to provide an air transport capability between naval bases in metropolitan France and Africa. The unit's initial equipment consisted of three French flying boats that had survived the war – the Latécoère 611 prototype, Breguet Br.730 No 1 and a Breguet Bizerte. Service entry of the Germanic Do 24s presented some difficulties, but in March 1945 the first long-distance flight to Dakar was made.

In May 1945 *Flottille* 4S, which was based at Cuers-Pierre with Supermarine Walrus amphibians, began to convert to the Do 24, and after working up the unit left for Karouba, near Bizerte in Tunisia, on 17 December 1945.

Aéronavale units were re-designated on 1 January 1946, and, confusingly, *Flottille* 4S at Karouba became *Flottille* 9F, while *Flottille* 9FTr became *Escadrille de Servitude* (second-line squadron) 30S. Karouba-based 9F had 12 Do 24s, which it operated principally in the anti-submarine role, while also taking on transport and rescue work. The oddball French flying boats of 30S were transferred to long-range transport squadron 33S, leaving 30S to focus exclusively on shorter-range transport and search and rescue with its complement of eight Do 24s.

In April 1946 *Escadrille* 20S was raised at Ajaccio-Aspretto, on Corsica – a small search and rescue outfit with a few Do 24s and crews. Do 24s were also used by the seaplane flying school at Hourtin, the *École de Pilotage d'Hydravions* or *Escadrille* 53S. Another Do 24 was assigned to the *Aéronavale*'s *Commission d'Etudes Pratiques d'Aéronautique* (Commission for the Practical Study of Aviation) test centre at St-Raphaël.

Do 24 operations were not without accidents. On 20 December 1945 Do 24 No 1 crashed into the sea near the Deux Frères rocks after taking off from St-Mandrier, killing the crew and 13 of 15 trainee mechanics that were on board. Do 24 No 15, coded 9F-6, disappeared on a rescue training flight from Karouba on 8 February 1946 with eight men on board. Another Dornier crashed at Aspretto in October 1946, and *Escadrille* 30S Do 24 No 8 was lost due to a fuel vapour explosion on board in March 1946.

The *Aéronavale*'s waterborne aviation was still in a poor condition, with the war in French Indochina

Escadrille de Servitude 30, initially designated *Flottille* 9FTr (Transport), was the first *Aéronavale* unit to receive the Do 24. It was based at St-Mandrier, near Toulon. The squadron's role soon changed from long-distance transport to shorter-range communications, as well as search and rescue (*T Postma*)

Almost a sesquiplane in this unusual view, this *Flottille* 9F flying boat shows off the Do 24's sharp bow. A radar antenna is fitted on top of the wing, the radar operator being seated in the dorsal turret space (*P Dupont*)

Whereas the rescue aircraft of the *Escadrilles de Servitude* were usually painted white, the maritime reconnaissance machines of *Flottille* 9F at Bizerte-Karouba wore a pale olive green. 9F's swan badge was made official and put on a coat of arms by 1947, as displayed here by aircraft 9F-5 at Karouba (*P Dupont*)

(Vietnam) – in which the Do 24 took no part – draining resources. Fuel was in short supply, and serviceability of the Dornier fleet was low due to spares shortages. *Flottille* 9F logged a total of only 800 flight hours during 1947, and in June 1948 the Do 24 fleet was temporarily grounded due to problems with the Bramo Fafnir engines. The morale in *Escadrille* 30S got a boost a month later. During the morning of 21 July Vickers Wellington LP650 of the *Aéronavale* ditched into the sea during a liaison flight from Réghaïa, near Algiers, to Istres with five crew and eight passengers on board. Despite high waves and a strong wind, a Do 24 of 30S was able to land and rescue four passengers and the Wellington's radio operator, Sgt Roger Peyrichou. The remaining eight men drowned, however.

Flottille 9F temporarily deployed to Hourtin, in France, in May 1948 to take part in the naval exercise *Cachalot*. On 16 June Do 24 9F-6 was lost when it had to land in the sea off Brest and was driven onto rocks. A short while later a second aircraft from the unit shed a whole propeller in flight while flying to Brittany from Tunisia. A temporary flight ban grounded the Dornier fleet after the exercise had ended.

Not surprisingly, Michael Laurent, who served with 9F as a radio operator, says that the Do 24 had a 'rather bad reputation', suffering from

On 16 June 1948 a Do 24 of *Flottille* 9F was thrown onto the rocks near Brest after making an emergency landing off Ushant Island. Although based in Tunisia, the unit had flown to Brittany for an exercise (*P Dupont*)

various problems that included the leaking of fuel into the cabin, thus making it impossible for the crew to operate some of the equipment – or to smoke on board. Evacuating the aircraft through the gun positions was difficult, and the shielding of electrical cables was a constant worry. 'I think that the Do 24 was designed for use on freshwater lakes', explains Seaman mechanic Christian Beltran. 'All the controls were electric, and they were always malfunctioning. This never happened with the hydraulic controls of the PBY. At Hourtin the Do 24s did not go unserviceable as often as at Karouba'.

By the autumn of 1948 *Escadrille* 30S was down to only two serviceable Do 24s and crews. The unit had given up its transport role to focus on the search and rescue mission. Its Corsican sister unit, 20S, lost another Do 24 on 2 June 1949. Aircraft No 22 departed St-Mandrier to fly back to Ajaccio, but it soon had to turn back with engine problems. The pilot, PO Jean Bohain, was forced to crash land in heavy seas near Port Cros Island. The flying boat went down with Bohain still at the controls, although the remaining eight people on board survived.

By early 1950 20S had been disbanded and amalgamated with 30S at St-Mandrier. Readiness was improved by this measure, and 34 hours were flown in two days as the French freighter *Sainte Anne*, on its way from Algiers to Toulon, disappeared without trace in March. Soon thereafter, though, the French navy decided to terminate Do 24 overhauls and axe the aircraft as their remaining flying hours ran out. *Flottille* 9F duly began its conversion to a very different aeroplane – the SB2C Helldiver – in April 1951, and its Do 24s went to *Escadrille* 30S, which was itself disbanded in January 1952. The last few French Do 24s served with the seaplane flying school, now based at Karouba. Five aircraft – Nos 6, 27, 31, 35 and 37 – were finally offered for sale to Spain, which still operated the Do 24, and were inspected at Karouba by a Spanish delegation in April 1953. Despite positive findings, the deal fell though and the surviving French Do 24s were scrapped in May 1954.

SPAIN

The Spanish association with the Do 24 came about during World War 2 when there was talk of a neutral air-sea rescue service being established in the Baleares that would help both Allied and Axis personnel. Although nothing came of it, in early 1944 the Germans, wishing to save manpower, agreed to transfer 12 Do 24T-3s to Spain. In April of that year personnel from the Pollensa seaplane base on Mallorca travelled to the Étang de Berre in occupied France for a Do 24 conversion course with *Seenotstaffel* 3.

The first Do 24 for Spain (a brand new aircraft built by Fokker) arrived at Pollensa on 30 May 1944. It was flown by Comandante Carlos Pombo Somoza, who would command the Spanish rescue squadron. The flying boat went into action on the very day it arrived in Mallorca, as a German aircraft was reported to have been shot down off Port-Vendres, near the Franco-Spanish border. Its pilot was picked up by a German lifeboat, however. On the way home the Do 24 was intercepted by a pair of RAF Beaufighters, whose crews correctly identified it as a neutral aircraft and duly left the seaplane alone. Although standard German camouflage was worn by the Do 24s, conspicuous Spanish and Red Cross markings were also applied. Civil registrations were initially carried, except by the last few machines that were not delivered until late 1944. With fighting in the Western Mediterranean now over, the flying boats took off their 'civilian jackets' and became regular military aeroplanes assigned to 53 *Grupo de Reconocimiento Lejano* (Long-Range Reconnaissance Group).

The Do 24s sometimes participated in exercises with the Spanish navy, such cooperation happening for the first time in November 1946 when three aircraft flew to El Ferrol, in Galicia. They returned home via Cádiz in December, thus having circumnavigated the Iberian Peninsula.

However, search and rescue around the Baleares remained the main role, and the individual aircraft were given names relating to the Virgin Mary, such as *Virgen del Pilar* and *Virgen de la Paloma*. This did not prevent these two aircraft from being lost in accidents in 1948, however, although there were no casualties. Horizontal yellow stripes added on the fuselages – which were later changed to white – led the Do 24s to be nicknamed '*Guardias Civiles*', as these Spanish policemen wore yellow belts on their green uniforms.

In September 1951 an intensive search was mounted for French DC-3 F-BEIZ, which had crashed into the sea en route from Perpignan to Oran – only bodies were found by the Spanish flying boats, however. On 4 February 1954, the four occupants of a Nord Martinet that also went missing on a flight between Perpignan and Algeria were found in their dinghy by a Do 24 and picked up by the Italian ship *Catherine Schiaffino*.

By then the Do 24s were weary and suffering from spares shortages. On 12 April 1953 aircraft HR.5-11 *Virgen de los Ojos Grandes* carried a Spanish delegation to Karouba, in Tunisia, for an inspection of five Do 24s offered for sale by the French. 'Our Lady with the Big Eyes' then continued on to St-Mandrier for a look at the available spares and Bramo engines. Despite the poor serviceability achieved by the French themselves, the delegation filed a positive report. Yet the deal fell through as the 1953 Pact

To emphasise their neutrality, the Spanish Do 24s initially wore civil registrations, but these gave way to military markings as soon as the war in the Western Mediterranean was over. Red crosses were still worn both on the fuselage and on top of the wing, however, and the rudders wore the Spanish national colours rather than the regular St Andrew's cross (*J Arráez Cerdá*)

of Madrid paved the way for American military aid to Franco's Spain. Seven Grumman SA-16A Albatross amphibians duly arrived on Mallorca the following year. The Falangist air force apparently found it difficult to part with its Heinkels, Junkers and Dorniers, however, and the Do 24s were kept in service with 51 *Escuadrilla de Salvamiento* alongside the SA-16s of 50 *Escuadrilla*. The squadron was later renumbered 58 *Escuadrilla*, and 804 *Escuadrilla* later still.

Two of the flying boats were lost in 1955, the first one exploding on the tarmac at Pollensa and the second breaking up in a rough landing following an engine failure on 5 August. An Albatross scrambled to come to the rescue while a fishing boat picked up three heavily wounded crewmen and the body of the radio operator. The three remaining crew members have never been found.

In 1958 four of the remaining six Do 24s were refurbished to continue in service, receiving the new serials HD.5-1 through -4. They got a new bare metal look in 1960. On 30 June 1965 the Do 24 performed its last rescue when HD.5-4 landed alongside the Israeli liner *Jerusalem* on a rough sea to pick up a child suffering from acute peritonitis. From August 1965, one Do 24 was cannibalised to keep the other three airworthy until they were finally retired from service on 20 November 1969.

HD.5-1 is currently preserved in the Netherlands Museum of Military Aviation in Soesterberg, painted as a Cyclone-powered Do 24K-1 X-24, while HD.5-2 resides in the *Museo del Aire* in Madrid and HD.5-3 is an exhibit in the Deutsches Museum's Flugwert Schleissheim, on the outskirts of Munich. Finally, the fuselage of HD.5-4 was used to produce the turbine-powered Do 24ATT amphibian.

HD.5-4 (formerly HR.5-12) was one of the final three Spanish Do 24s that soldiered on until 1969. Although their serviceability was questionable, in terms of seaworthiness they were considered superior to the HU-16 Albatross amphibians that had long since entered service as their replacements (*J Arráez Cerdá*)

APPENDICES

LUFTWAFFE AIR-SEA RESCUE Do 24 SQUADRONS

UNIT	UNIT DESIGNATION FROM SUMMER 1944	UNIT CODE FROM SPRING 1944	AREA OF OPERATIONS
Seenotstaffel 1	-	W4+.H	French Atlantic coast
Seenotstaffel 2	-	S5+.H	Channel coast, later Low Countries and Baltic
Seenotstaffel 3	-	M6+.L	Low Countries, later Western Mediterranean
Seenotstaffel 4	*Seenotstaffel* 80	U6+.M, later F4+.B	German Bight
Seenotstaffel 5	*Seenotstaffel* 51	P7+.N	Norway, later Arctic
Seenotstaffel 6		Q8+.A	Central Mediterranean
Seenotstaffel 7	*Seenotstaffel* 70	J9+.A	Eastern Mediterranean
Seenotstaffel 8		1M+..	Black Sea
Seenotstaffel 9	*Seenotstaffel* 81	3Y+.T, later G3+.S	Baltic
Seenotstaffel 10	*Seenotstaffel* 50	5W+.U	Arctic, later Norway

DUTCH NAVY Do 24 AIRCRAFT GROUPS

UNIT	AREA OF OPERATIONS AND MAIN EVENTS			
	DECEMBER 1941	JANUARY 1942	FEBRUARY 1942	MARCH 1942
GVT 1	West coast of Borneo (from 12/12)	To Surabaya and disbanded 1/1	-	-
GVT 2	Dutch New Guinea, Davao raid 23/12, destroyed 26/12	Reformed on PBY	-	-
GVT 3	Singapore (from 10/12), to Surabaya 31/12	Converted to PBY	-	-
GVT 4	In maintenance (from 12/12)	East coast of Borneo, to Surabaya 24/1, disbanded 27/1	-	-
GVT 5	Moluccas/Celebes, Davao raid 23/12, destroyed 26/12	Converted to PBY	-	-
GVT 6	East Java	West coast of Borneo, Kuching raids, to Surabaya 30/1	East Java, Battle of the Java Sea 27/2	To Broome 2/3, destroyed 3/3
GVT 7	East coast of Borneo, Miri raid 17/12	To Surabaya 3/1, South Celebes mid-January, Sawu Sea 30/1	Sawu Sea, destroyed 7/2, reformed Surabaya mid-February, Battle of the Java Sea 27/2	To Broome 2/3, destroyed 3/3
GVT 8	In maintenance (from 10/12), West Java/Sumatra 23/12	West Java/Sumatra	West Java/Sumatra, Bangka raid 24/2	Last aircraft destroyed 1/3

COLOUR PLATES

1
Do 24 V1 TJ+HR (Wk-Nr 760) of KGzbV 108 (See), based at Travemünde, Germany, April 1940
The V1 prototype was not the first Do 24 to fly, this distinction going to the V3 prototype of the Dutch Do 24K model (see Profile 2). Powered by weak Jumo diesels, the V1 and V2 could not convince the Reich Air Ministry of the Do 24's merits. Used as test beds by the E-Stelle Travemünde, both prototypes were rushed into service with KGzbV 108 (See) during Operation *Weserübung*, with the V1 flying the first supply mission into Narvik on 12 April 1940, piloted by Adolf Mlodoch. The flying boat was armed with a non-standard Rheinmetall-Borsig MG 204 20 mm cannon in a HD 151 turret and MG 15 machine guns in the open nose and tail positions.

2
Do 24 V3/Do 24K-1 X-1 (Wk-Nr 761) of the MLD, Surabaya-Morokrembangan, Java, January 1938
On order for the Dutch navy, the Cyclone-powered V3 prototype made the Do 24's maiden flight on 3 July 1937. The test programme was remarkably trouble-free, and X-1 was flying in the East Indies as a Do 24K-1 service aircraft by early 1938. The first 12 Do 24Ks had an Alkan machine gun turret in the dorsal position, rather than the SAMM cannon turret, and they were used mainly in training roles at the MLD's Morokrembangan complex. In February 1942 X-1 was assigned to GVT 7 for operational duties in the war against Japan. During the night of 3 March the aircraft was evacuated to Australia, only to be sunk by Zero-sens during their infamous raid on Roebuck Bay, Broome, the following morning.

3
Do 24K-1 X-32 (c/n 69) of the MLD, Aviolanda factory, Papendrecht, the Netherlands, September 1939
X-32 was the third Do 24 built in Holland, and the last one to be delivered wearing normal Dutch roundels, although red, white and blue rudders had been abolished in December 1938. In December 1941 this flying boat was assigned to GVT 7 at Tarakan, on the east coast of Dutch Borneo, and on the 17th it sank the Japanese destroyer *Shinonome*. Around the turn of the year X-32 rescued a total of 138 crewmen from the stricken ships *Ruth Alexander*, *Camphuys* and *Djirak*. The aircraft was destroyed by Japanese aircraft at Rote Island on 7 February 1942.

4
Do 24K-1 X-35 (c/n 72) of GVT 1, Surabaya-Morokrembangan, Java, 1940
Dutch military aircraft received orange triangle markings as of 1 October 1939. Rudders were also painted orange, but this was done away with in the East Indies in July 1941 when the fuselage triangles were reduced in size and the upper wing ones removed. Commanded by Lt Piet Jaapies, this GVT 1 aircraft guided the Dutch submarine *K XIV* into a successful attack against a Japanese convoy off Borneo on 23 December 1941. Like X-32, X-35 was destroyed in an air raid on Rote Island on 7 February 1942.

5
Do 24K-1 X-12 (Wk-Nr 772) of GVT 2, flown by Lt Adriaan Höfelt, Sorong, Netherlands New Guinea, December 1941
Built by the Swiss Dornier plant, X-12 was shipped to the East

Indies in September 1938 and deployed to Ambon with the first operational Do 24 group, GVT 3, in November. A new camouflage scheme of 'mud blue grey' and 'milky white' was introduced during 1941. X-12 was the first Do 24 to see action after the outbreak of the war in the Pacific, unsuccessfully attacking a Japanese schooner. On 23 December it took part in the MLD raid against Davao, in the Philippines, but three days later the flying boat was destroyed by Zero-sens at the forward base of Kalas, on Lake Tondano in the Celebes.

6
Do 24K-1 X-36 (c/n 73) of GVT 7, flown by Lt Jo Petschi, Lake Grati, East Java, February 1942
The last Do 24K-1 to be built, X-36 was allocated to GVT 1 in the South China Sea area in December 1941. It was damaged in an air raid at Pontaniak on the 20th, but repaired at Surabaya and sent back into action within days. In February 1942 X-36 was assigned to GVT 7. Making for Australia, the seaplane ended up at Eighty Mile Beach, in Western Australia, on 3 March, thus escaping the Japanese raid against Broome. However, having suffered damage when it hit a reef offshore, the seaplane could not be retrieved from this isolated location and therefore had to be destroyed by its crew.

7
Do 24K-1 X-24 (Wk-Nr 785) of the MLD Australia Detachment, flown by Lt Bastiaan Sjerp, Rose Bay, Sydney, New South Wales, June 1942
Shipped to the East Indies in May 1939, X-24 was used as a training aircraft at Surabaya during the first weeks of the Pacific War. It rescued 54 American sailors from the freighter USAT *Liberty* on 11 January 1942. Assigned to GVT 7, it made for Australia on 2 March. The only surviving cannon turret Do 24, it was then used for flights to Dutch New Guinea on behalf of the Netherlands Forces Intelligence service, in particular to the Wisselmeren (Panai Lakes) outpost led by Dr Victor de Bruijn. Plagued by breakdowns and having very poor fuel economy, 'Ouwe Lobbes' (old, big friendly dog) was given to the RAAF in late 1943. It was eventually put in storage at Lake Boga, and ended up at a playground near Blackhalls Park on Lake Macquarie in 1950.

8
Do 24N-1 D-AP+DA (Wk-Nr 0002) of *Seenotflugkommando* 4, flown by *Flugkapitän* Karl Born, Norderney, Germany, August 1940
After the conquest of Holland, two captured Do 24s of the Dutch navy were sent to the *Seenotdienst* base on Norderney Island for operational trials. At this point, *Seenotdienst* aircraft were still unarmed and painted white with Red Cross markings, civil registrations and the non-canted swastika used by civil government services. Note that rescue hatches were not yet installed in the aircraft. Flown by Karl Born, D-AP+DA was wrecked during a rescue action on 17 August 1940.

9
Do 24N-1 KD+GA (Wk-Nr 0001) of *Seenotstaffel* 6, Syracuse, Sicily, April 1941
Formerly D-AE+AV in the white Red Cross livery, the very first Do 24 of the *Seenotdienst* was among the Do 24Ns flying from Sicily with

Seenotstaffel 6 by early 1941. Although little involved in the invasions of Yugoslavia and Greece, they initially wore conspicuous yellow Balkan campaign markings. In November 1941 KD+GA was operating from the Gulf of Bumba, Libya, providing rescue cover for Axis aircraft targeting the besieged port of Tobruk. The aircraft was unserviceable when Allied Operation *Crusader* forced the Axis on the retreat, and the seaplane was destroyed to prevent it from falling into enemy hands.

10
Do 24N-1 KK+UP (Wk-Nr 0011) of *Seenotstaffel* 6, Syracuse, Sicily, December 1942
KK+UP was one of the longest-lasting Do 24Ns. On 1 May 1942 this *Seenotstaffel* 6 aircraft, commanded by Leutnant Ernst Warganz, rescued the crew of Do 24T-2 CH+EZ, which had been wrecked in a rough landing off Vittoria, Sicily. Photographed in Tunis harbour in late 1942, KK+UP eventually fell to the guns of Flt Lt Eric Norman's Spitfire VC of No 72 Sqn near Malta on 19 December 1942. The flying boat was wearing standard seaplane splinter camouflage of two shades of green over light blue undersurfaces at the time of its demise. Markings were also standard, with a white Mediterranean theatre band worn around the tail.

11
Do 24T-1 KK+UT (Wk-Nr 0015) of *Seenotstaffel* 2, Brest-Poulmic, France, September 1941
The second airframe of the Bramo Fafnir-powered Do 24T series, KK+UT was delivered in April 1941 and was in service with *Seenotstaffel* 1 at Brest by the summer. The T-1 and T-2 models retained the French SAMM dorsal turret selected by the Dutch navy. Repaired after breaking its tail at one point, KK+UT had a relatively long service life. Whilst on its way from the squadron's *Aussenstelle* (detachment) at Hourtin to its main base at Brest-Poulmic, it was shot down near Dreux on 9 February 1944.

12
Do 24T-1 KK+VA (Wk-Nr 0022) of *Seenotstaffel* 5, Stavanger, Norway, 1942
Another one of the 11 Do 24T-1s delivered to the Luftwaffe, KK+VA spent its operational career in Norway. Originally flown by *Seenotstaffel* 5, this machine was assigned to *Seenotstaffel* 10 in the Arctic when the Norwegian air-sea rescue unit was split in July 1942. On 26 May 1943 KK+VA was loaned to the *Führerkurierstaffel* (Führer's Courier Squadron) as a transport for the Todt construction organisation. On 13 June it was shot down off Karmøy, near Haugesund, by Mosquito II DZ744 of No 333 (Norwegian) Sqn, the RAF fighter being flown by Lt Knut Skavhaugen and PO Jan Erling Heide. The crew of pilot Feldwebel Josef Gibisch and his passengers were killed, except the radio operator, Unteroffizier Kurt Fritsch, who was wounded.

13
Do 24T-2 CM+IS (Wk-Nr 0053) of *Seenotstaffel* 3, Amsterdam-Schellingwoude, Holland, 1942
Like most Do 24s, CM+IS was built by Aviolanda in Papendrecht, Holland. After outfitting and acceptance in Germany, this aircraft returned to the Netherlands, as Schellingwoude, in Amsterdam, was the *de facto* main base of *Seenotstaffel* 3 until early 1943, when the squadron was moved to the south coast of France. CM+IS rescued – and captured – the Halifax crew of Sqn Ldr Francis Peter Hewitt off Vlissingen (Flushing) on 1 August 1942. The aircraft is wearing the badge of *Seenotstaffel* 3 – a gull carrying a lifebelt on a blue shield.

14
Do 24T-2 CM+IG (Wk-Nr 0041) of *Seenotstaffel* 8, flown by Unteroffizier Ludwig Gosepath, Ak-Metschet (Chornomorske), Crimea, July 1942
Delivered to the *Seenotdienst* on 29 March 1942, CM+IG was flown to the Black Sea coast on 7 April and completed its maiden rescue mission one week later, fruitlessly searching for a ditched Ju 88 of *Wettererkundungsstaffel* 76. On 6 May CM+IG picked up four crew of a He 111 torpedo-bomber from 6./KG 26. Late at night on 9 July the flying boat crashed into the shore at Mamaia after a ferry flight from the Crimea on two engines. CM+IG was painted in standard camouflage and markings with a yellow Eastern Front band, and the skull on a black shield badge of *Seenotstaffel* 8 worn on the starboard side of the nose. This unit marking has been confused in the past with the very similar badge of 3./*Küstenfliegergruppe* 106. This maritime reconnaissance unit never flew the Do 24, however.

15
Do 24T-2 CH+EV (Wk-Nr 0030) of *Seenotstaffel* 7, flown by Feldwebel Wilhelm Lange, Souda Bay, Crete, July 1942
Many *Seenotdienst* Do 24s wore names, and in the case of *Seenotstaffel* 7 in Greece, the *Staffelkapitän* chose to honour fallen comrades. CH+EV was named *Wilhelm Arndt* after a pilot who was killed in the crash of sister aircraft CH+EY during its delivery flight to Athens on 17 January 1942. Leutnant Arndt had been flying CH+EV during the previous month. Later on, this Do 24T-2 was often flown by Feldwebel Wihelm Lange. With Lange at the controls, CH+EV rescued a He 111 crew in February 1942, operating from Souda Bay, where 7. *Staffel* maintained an important detachment. Three men from a Ju 88 were picked up by Lange's CH+EV crew on 10 July during the First Battle of El Alamein. Two days later, in the port of Mersa Matruh, Egypt, the aircraft was damaged beyond practical repair in an Allied naval bombardment.

16
Do 24T-2 CM+IT (Wk-Nr 0054) of *Seenotstaffel* 7, flown by Oberfeldwebel Hans Sost, Syracuse, Sicily, December 1942
Entering service on 17 June 1942, CM+IT was the first Do 24 assembled by the Fokker factory in Amsterdam as the Germans sought to accelerate production in view of the heavy attrition being suffered by the *Seenotstaffeln*. Mauled during the Battle of Malta, 6. *Staffel* at Syracuse was particularly hard-pressed in 1942. Its sister squadron in Greece lent a hand in the form of CM+IT, which was detached to Syracuse to lighten 6. *Staffel*'s workload. On 17 December, however, the aircraft collided with a mast during its departure for Tunisia with a cargo of fuel – pilot Oberfeldwebel Hans Sost, observer Oberleutnant Hans Kurz and their entire crew were killed. The flying boat was named *Johann Wehling* after a flight engineer of 7. *Staffel* who had gone before them on 17 February 1942.

17
Do 24T-2 CM+IA (Wk-Nr 0035) of *Seenotstaffel* 9, Friedrichshafen, Germany, February 1943
Raised to cover the Baltic flank of Operation *Barbarossa*, *Seenotstaffel* 9 had adopted a training and evaluation role for the other air-sea rescue squadrons at Kiel–Holtenau by late 1941. Severe frost in the Baltic prompted a winter training camp on Lake Constance, and this was repeated during the next winter of 1942-43. CM+IA was one of the unit's Do 24s temporarily based at Friedrichshafen at this time. It is painted in standard markings only,

unlike many 9. *Staffel* aircraft that wore the squadron badge and names of ships.

18

Do 24T-2 CM+IV (Wk-Nr 0056) of *Seenotstaffel* 8, flown by Leutnant Werner Lange, Ortasli-See (Lake Tobechiskoye), Crimea, February 1943

CM+IV was delivered to the *Seenotdienst* on 11 June 1942, and it reached 8. *Staffel* at Constanţa–Mamaia on 26 July. On 21 February 1943 this aircraft reconnoitred the Vityazevski Lake as the seaplane airhead for the Kuban airlift, during which operation it rescued a Ju 52/3m See seaplane crew. Later in 1943 CM+IV was transferred to *Seenotstaffel* 4 in the German Bight. On 23 August the flying boat, having landed on the North Sea to pick up two British airmen, was destroyed by the gunners of a 303rd BG B-17. While in the Black Sea CM+IV wore 8. *Staffel's* skull badge and the yellow theatre band. The last letter of the *Stammkennzeichen* military registration was painted yellow.

19

Do 24T-2 CH+EX (Wk-Nr 0032) of *Seenotstaffel* 7, flown by Unteroffizier Hans Lieber, Athens-Phaleron, Greece, October 1943

CH+EX belonged to *Seenotstaffel* 7 in Greece from early 1942, and it was often the mount of the *Staffelkapitän*, Hans Tretter. During March 1943 the aircraft was in the Black Sea to participate in the Kuban airlift, surviving combat with six Yak fighters on 18 March. Following Italy's surrender in September, CH+EX was involved in the takeover of the Greek islands by German forces. On 29 October it was lost in a takeoff accident at Naxos, six crew and three passengers losing their lives. At this time CH+EX wore 7. *Staffel's* later badge – an angel on a cloud, looking through a telescope – and the name *Karl Lierse* after a radio operator who had been killed in action on 17 February 1942.

20

Do 24T-3 M6+IL of *Seenotstaffel* 3, Berre, France, mid-1944

Produced from August 1942, the T-3 was numerically by far the most important Do 24 model, featuring an HD 151 turret in the dorsal position. Through attrition, the Do 24T-3 had largely replaced the older marks by war's end. Squadron codes were allocated to the *Seenotstaffeln* in the spring of 1944, replacing the four-letter *Stammkenzeichen* on the Do 24s. 3. *Staffel* used M6+.L codes, with the individual aircraft letter painted yellow. This unit was based on the south coast of France from late 1942 until 15 August 1944 – the day of the Allied Operation *Anvil* landings in southern France.

21

Do 24T-3 W4+BH (Wk-Nr 1007) of *Seenotstaffel* 1, flown by Feldwebel Heinrich Reif, Biscarrosse-Hourtiquets, France, August 1944

Built by SNCAN in Sartrouville, CI+GU received the *Seenotstaffel* 1 tactical code W4+BH in the spring of 1944 – the individual aircraft letter 'B' was painted white. Two months after D-Day 1. *Staffel* was ordered to withdraw from its final French base, the Hourtiquet seaplane station on Lake Biscarosse, with its surviving Do 24s and Breguet Bizertes. During the departure, under the cover of darkness and radio silence, Feldwebel Reif's machine collided with Do 24T-3 W4+DH (Wk-Nr 1101) and both damaged flying boats were scuttled in the lake. The wrecks were salvaged in the 1980s.

22

Do 24T-3 Q8+AE (Wk-Nr 2101) of *Seenotstaffel* 70, flown by Feldwebel Günther Weisshuhn, Athens-Phaleron, Greece, September 1944

Q8+.E squadron codes belonged to *Seenotstaffel* 6 in Italy, lately based in Venice. However, *Seenotstaffel* 70 in Athens did not bother to change them when it absorbed the surviving aircraft of both 6. and 8. *Staffel* in the summer of 1944. Q8+AE spent an eventful couple of months in the Aegean, as detailed in Chapter 5. Following the unit's withdrawal from Athens, Q8+AE eventually crashed during a night landing at Salonica. Although this Fokker-built flying boat no longer wore the Mediterranean theatre band, the last letter of its code was painted white and a white spiral adorned the propeller spinners.

23

Do 24T-3 CM+RY (Wk-Nr 3343) of *Seenotstaffel* 81, Nest, Pomerania, October 1944

Built by Aviolanda but assembled by Fokker in Amsterdam, CM+RY served with *Seenotstaffel* 9 and 81 in the Baltic in 1944. Based at Nest, near Köslin (Koszalin), the fairly new aircraft had not yet received a squadron code when it was hijacked by flight engineer Heinz Roesch and his Estonian girlfriend on 31 October 1944. Roesch managed a perfectly good landing off Sölvesborg, in Sweden, and CM+RY eventually entered service with the F2 wing of the Swedish air force.

24

Do 24T-3 A3+EE (Wk-Nr unknown) of 3./KG 200, at Bug on Rügen, Germany, March 1945

German use of the Do 24 was almost exclusively restricted to the various *Seenotdienst* units and some ad hoc transport squadrons. In 1944-45, however, the secretive *Kampfgeschwader* 200 operated two machines for the insertion of spies or saboteurs into the Soviet hinterland. 3./KG 200 seaplanes mounted missions from bases in Finland during the summer of 1944, but the presence of the Do 24s there is unconfirmed. A3+EE was flown from Bug to Schleswig in May 1945, and it lay abandoned there after the war had ended. The flying boat had been painted for nocturnal operations, with black undersurfaces and low visibility national markings.

25

Do 24T-3 (Wk-Nr unknown) of *Seenotstaffel* 81, Schleswig, July 1945

Seenotstaffel 81 was the last operational squadron of the *Seenotdienst* (*Luft*), participating in the evacuation of German refugees from Pillau and other Baltic ports threatened by the Red Army. On 5 May 1945 the squadron flew from Bug on Rügen to Guldborg, Denmark, in order to continue its duties – German forces in Denmark surrendered on the same day, however. The *Staffel* flew one more mission on 18 June 1945, transporting wounded German soldiers from Denmark to Schleswig, with British consent. Swastikas and aircraft codes were painted out for this flight and Red Cross markings applied on the fuselage. The gun turrets were also removed at some point.

26

Do 24K-1 A49-1/DQ-D (Wk-Nr 765) of No 41 Sqn, RAAF, detached to No 8 Communications Unit, Kiriwina, Tobriand Islands, March 1944

The Dutch Do 24s taken over by the RAAF did not operate in combat roles, but they did fly into operational areas around eastern New Guinea, mainly as transport flying boats. Latterly undertaking the search and rescue role, A49-1 arrived at Kiriwina, in the Tobriand Islands, on 16 March 1944, relieving A49-3. It rescued an A-20 Boston crew the following day. Operational service of the RAAF Do 24s ended some weeks later in May. Formerly X-5, A49-1 was one of the first production Do 24s, delivered from Friedrichshafen to Holland on 18 March 1938.

27
Do 24T-3 or Tp 24 (Wk-Nr 3343) of the F2 wing, *Flygvapnet*, Hägernas, Sweden, circa 1946

Flown to Sweden by deserting flight engineer Heinz Roesch, this is the same aircraft as depicted in Profile 23 after service entry with the F2 wing *(Roslagens Flygflottilj)*. The uppersurfaces were painted in a black-green different from the German or standard Swedish colours. Used in its familiar search and rescue role, the flying boat was subsequently stripped of all paint and given a bare metal look. Replaced by PBY-5A Canso amphibians, it was scrapped in 1951.

28
Do 24 (c/n unknown) 20S-4 of *Escadrille de Servitude* 20, *Aéronavale*, Ajaccio-Aspretto, Corsica, circa 1949

The Sartrouville production line resumed work after the liberation of France, and some 40 Do 24s were built for the *Aéronavale*. Although basically unchanged from the Do 24T-3, the seaplanes incorporated some French or British equipment. The gun turrets were often removed or changed around, and this machine seems to have the German rear turret in the nose position! It was one of only a handful of Do 24s flown by *Escadrille de Servitude* 20, a Corsica-based rescue outfit, and it wore the badge of the French navy's air-sea rescue service – a dolphin jumping through a life buoy.

29
Do 24T-3 HR.5-7 (Wk-Nr 5341) of 53 *Grupo de Reconocimiento Lejano*, 51 *Regimiento de Hidros, Ejército del Aire*, Pollensa, Mallorca, 1946

Twelve German Do 24T-3s were transferred to Spain in 1944, including this machine, the Luftwaffe service history of which is unknown. Originally registered EC-DAG, it was soon militarised, with ample national insignia and Red Cross markings and the name *Virgen del Camino*. HR.5-7 was one of the Do 24s that remained in service into the late 1960s, its serial changing to HD.5-2 in 1965. The flying boat is currently preserved in the *Museo del Aire* at Madrid's Cuatro Vientos airfield.

30
Do 24T-3 HD.5-1 (Wk-Nr 3387), 804 *Escuadrilla de Salvamiento, Ejército del Aire*, Pollensa, Mallorca, 1966

Another long-serving Do 24 of the Spanish *Servicio Aéreo de Rescate* in the Balearic Islands, Wk-Nr 3387 was originally allocated the serial HR.5-11 and the name *Virgen de los Ojos Grandes*. Note the small nose cupola fitted to this machine. Finally retired in November 1969, HD.5-1 was displayed within the RAF Museum at Hendon for many years but it is now in the Netherlands Museum of Military Aviation, Soesterberg, impersonating Cyclone-powered Do 24K-1 X-24 of the Dutch navy.

BIBLIOGRAPHY

Arraéz Cerdá, Juan, *Los Dornier Do 24T-3 'Guardias Civiles'*, Serga, Spain, July-October 2000

Beauvais, Heinrich and others, *Flugerprobungsstellen bis 1945: Johannisthal, Lipezk, Rechlin, Travemünde, Tarnewitz, Peenemünde-West*, Bernard & Graefe, Germany, 1998

Born, Karl, *Rettung zwischen den Fronten: Seenotdienst der deutschen Luftwaffe 1939-1945*, Mittler & Sohn, Germany, 1996

De Bruijn, J V, *Het verdwenen volk*, Van Holkema & Warendorf, the Netherlands, 1978

De Zwart, André, www.dornier24.com, 1999-2006

Geldhof, N, *Verkennen en bewaken: Dornier Do 24K vliegboten van de Marineluchtvaartdienst*, Maritime History Section of the Ministry of Defence, the Netherlands, 1979

Kühn, Volkmar, *Der Seenotdienst der deutschen Luftwaffe 1939-1945*, Motorbuch, Germany, 1978

Müller, Wolfgang, *Seenotgruppe 81/Ostsee 1944-45,* Sundwerbung, Germany, 2005

Roba, J L and Craciunoiu, C, *Seaplanes over the Black Sea: German and Rumanian Operations 1941-1944*, Modelism, Rumania, 1995

Stemmer, Gerhard, *Seenotdienst (Air/Sea Rescue Service)*, Luftwaffe Verband, USA, January-July 2004

Thürling, Horst, *Die 7. Seenotstaffel 1941-1944: Eine Chronik*, Rudower Panorama Verlag, Germany, 1997

Van Wijngaarden, Pieter and Staal, Prudent, *Dornier Do 24: Herinneringen aan een legendarische vliegboot*, Bonneville, the Netherlands, 1992

Verheijke, Emma (editor), *Broome: 3 March 1942–3 March 2012*, Embassy of the Kingdom of the Netherlands/Museum of Western Australia, Australia, 2012

Womack, Tom, *The Dutch Naval Air Force Against Japan: The Defense of the Netherlands East Indies, 1941–1942*, McFarland & Company, USA, 2006

INDEX